The 7 Steps to A Successful Marriage

The 7 Steps to A Successful Marriage

By Vic and May Victor

All scripture quotations unless otherwise marked are taken from the New King James Version of the Holy Bible. Copyright © 1979, 1980, 1982, Thomas Nelson, Inc., Publishers

GOD'S WORD is a copyrighted work of God's Word to the Nations. Quotations are used by permission. Copyright 1995 by God's Word to the Nations. All rights reserved.

Holy Bible, New International Version ®, NIV®. Copyright © 1973, 1978, 1984, 2011 by Biblica, Inc.®. Used by permission. All rights reserved worldwide

Copyright © 2012 by Victor & May Victor

No part of this publication may be reproduced, stored in a retrieval system or transmitted in any way by any means, electronics, mechanical, photocopy, recording or otherwise, without the prior permission of the author except as provided by USA copyright law.

DEDICATION

We give God all the glory for bringing us together and for keeping us together. There is no perfect marriage but we have a perfect God. Holy Spirit this is for you and all those aspiring to succeed in their marriage.

ACKNOWLEDGEMENT

We acknowledge the hand of the Holy Spirit for opening our eyes of understanding. The things that are revealed belong to our children and us.

Thanks to Pastors Joe and Cordelia Nwokocha of the household of God at Kingsway Family Church Polokwane, South Africa and Pastors Joel and Fumi Uzoma of Redeemed Christian Church of God, Daysprings, Houston Texas for the invitation to share the word of God and the inspiration to write about God's kind of marriage.

To our fans, friends and followers of Twogether for Ever on Face book, twitter and Blackberry Messenger, thank you for giving us the opportunity to serve the Kingdom. We set out to minister to you but you have made it a church where we all minister to each other. You bless us daily with your likes, comments and dissents. We love you all.

TABLE OF CONTENTS

DEDICATION v

ACKNOWLEDGEMENT vii

Introduction 1

Prelude 8

Chapter 1 Lay The Right Foundation 11

Chapter 2 Marry For The Right Purpose 24

Chapter 3 Choose The Right Partner 34

Chapter 4 Know Your Role In Marriage 41

Chapter 5 Follow The Process Of Marriage 55

Chapter 6 Set Boundaries For Your Marriage And Defend It 70

Chapter 7 Hunker Down For The Long Journey 82

Chapter 8 The 5 Steps To Remaking A Messed-Up Marriage 86

Chapter 9 Epilogue 95

Introduction

Marriage is designed by God to be the best experience of your lifetime. It is certainly the most significant event in your life other than your choice of a higher power. The scripture compares establishing a home to building a house.

"Through wisdom a house is built, And by understanding it is established; By knowledge the rooms are filled With all precious and pleasant riches.

" Proverbs 24:3-4.

The 7 Steps to A Successful Marriage

"Unless the LORD builds the house, They labor in vain who build it; Unless the LORD guards the city, The watchman stays awake in vain.

" Psalm 127:1-2

Marriage is, therefore, like a building. In building a house, you must start from the foundation. The kind of foundation you build determines the stability of the house you are building. Recently the Lord opened my eyes to see the problem of marriages today. People want to build their marriage without laying the proper foundation. Others lay a Christ-centered foundation but decide to build a Hollywood marriage or marriage according to the world on that foundation. It will not work. *The 7 Steps to A Successful Marriage* will help you to identify all the available foundations and determine the right foundation for a Successful Marriage.

Marriage is also like a long distance journey and choosing a marriage partner is like choosing your driving partner for the lifetime journey. Can you imagine traveling on a long distance journey in a car with the wrong buddy? I can imagine it, and some of us do have the wrong driving partner, some have the right partner but are driving the wrong car, some are headed in the wrong direction and while others have everything right but they still can't get along in the car.

In spite of all this missteps marriage is still the best thing that can happen to any person. If God said it is not good for a

The 7 Steps to A Successful Marriage

man (and by implication a woman) to be alone, you better believe that it is certainly better to be married. A man of God once said that if you are not saved you live in hell when you die; if you marry the wrong person, you live in hell here in your house; but if you are not saved and marry the wrong person, you are doomed here on earth and after life. The 7 Steps to A Success Marriage provides a definitive guide to finding the right person and enjoying the ride to your destiny.

Marriage provides the platform for the pursuit of our purpose here on earth and the fulfillment of our destiny. Marriage gives us the comfort and the companionship that each of us needs to face the challenges of life. In defining the role of the woman in a marriage relationship, *The 7 Steps to A successful Marriage* broke down the word "HELPER" into an acronym as follows:

>H=to hold the man,
>
>E= to Embrace the man;
>
>L= to labor with the man;
>
>P= to pray and play with the man;
>
>E= Encourage the man;
>
>R= to rescue the man.

Let me also add that the man is required to LOVE his wife unto death.

Your marriage is very important to God because it is the cornerstone of God's plan to establish His kingdom on earth and extend it in heaven. God, the maker of marriage understood the complex nature of marriage and in response to

The 7 Steps to A Successful Marriage

that laid down a step-by-step process to His ideal marriage. *The 7 Steps to A Successful Marriage* is a reenactment of those steps to a blissful marriage. It is a review of the steps from the contemplation of marriage to conclusion of marriage.

I did not realize how much the word "step" has lost its meaning until I started writing this introduction. It is now always used in association with other words and surprisingly its more relevant in the manufacturing world than any other place. A Step is "an advance or a movement made by raising the foot and bringing it down elsewhere (2): a combination of foot or foot and body movements constituting a unit or a repeated pattern (3): manner of walking. (Webster). Other than that definition, the word step refers to the distance between two places, the sound of the foot and the space between one foot and the other. In this sense "The 7 Steps" are the seven movements toward the direction of a successful marriage. Each one of these steps gets you closer to your marital bliss.

The 7 Steps to A Successful Marriage is a step-by-step guide to your successful marriage. It is not "the 7 secrets", "the 7 keys", "the 7 principles" or "the 7 wisdoms". All these words suggest a theoretical formulation of a process to a set goal. It is not a "what to do" alone, but a combination of what to do and how to do it. You get the best result when you follow the steps methodically because the foundation steps stabilize the rest of the process. Jumping any of the processes will make the marriage more challenging.

The number '7' is the number for completion. God created the world in six days and rested on the seventh day. The 7 Steps to A Successful Marriage mirrors that structure in that it is actually a six-step process and a final resting step. That's why the last step is titled "Hunker Down For the Long

The 7 Steps to A Successful Marriage

Journey". It is a long and sometime arduous journey with unimaginable rewards of friendship, companionship and fulfillment.

One of the things that my father taught me while growing up is never to mess with someone's daughter. At that time I understood it only in the sense of sleeping with a girl or promising what I couldn't deliver but I see the relevance of that admonition today. Fortunately for me the best decision that I ever made in life was the most important decision. Choosing my wife as my life partner has proved to be the best decision that I could have made in that phase of my life. After 23 years of marriage it is getting better every day.

Please understand that your marriage, like every other marriage is the battle ground the supernatural forces. This is a fact that is not necessarily a new revelation. Right from the beginning, marriage has been the focus of all kinds of devilish machination. In the book of Genesis we see the cunning serpent using the marriage of Adam and Eve to advance his course. He encouraged one half of the team to rebel against God and by seducing Eve, it made it easier to convince Adam. The result was a failed marriage, a failed destiny, a lost status as a man of dominion, and a forfeited paradise as in the Garden of Eden.

Today that battle rages on and the devil's weapon of warfare is still the same- disobedience. Whenever we go away from the principles laid down by God and do our own thing or do other people's suggestions, we pay dearly for it. Our peace is accentuated, our progress is delayed and our destiny is truncated. Nothing sets a man or woman backward more than a failed marriage. It's like starting life all over at whatever age the marriage failed. You don't have to wait until it's your turn.

The 7 Steps to A Successful Marriage

Follow The 7 Steps to A Successful Marriage and you will get to your dream marriage.

Now we understand that some may read these 7 steps and wonder where or how they fit in, because they have taken a step or two out of sequence. Obviously some are establishing their marriage without first establishing a firm foundation. Some established a foundation alright but it is the wrong foundation. And yet, there are those who are confused, they started their marriage as a Christian marriage, then got carried away by the pressures of the world and now they are building their marriage according to the world. If you are one of those who have not followed "The 7 Steps" in your marriage or you followed the steps but not in the right order, this book is for you.

You may have chosen the right partner but laid the wrong foundation, this book will help you get back on track. Marriage involves two individuals and sometimes a marriage fails because one of the parties failed do his/her own part. Sometimes we were not matured enough to appreciate the seriousness of marriage before we took the vows of marriage. That's ok. I certainly did not know as much as I know now when I made my vows. Some of us got married before meeting the Lord and accepting His teachings. There is hope for all who desire to be successful in their marriage. We do not believe that there is a hopeless marriage.

God is a God of second chances and He knows our limitations and our makeup. He already knew that we may fail for one reason or the other so He has made provisions for our forgiveness and reconciliation with him. There is nothing too broken for God to repair just as there is no marriage too messed up for God to fix. God is a specialist in messed up marriages.

The 7 Steps to A Successful Marriage

He understands that we are frail and marriages fail for several reasons including some that are not our fault. The steps to building a successful marriage are the same steps for rebuilding a failed marriage except that the mindset is different. For each of the seven steps we have provided a "Step back and Step forward" process to get back on track.

Prelude

"For this reason a man shall leave his father and mother and cleave to his wife. And they shall become one flesh"

Genesis 2:24.

In the summer of 2001, my wife and I did something remarkable. We took our young family of five and Grandma on a journey across the United States of America. At that time Stephanie our only daughter was 9, Victor Jr. our first son was 7 and Tochi the baby of the family was 3 years old. The goal was to have fun traveling and seeing America. We agreed that the best way for us to really see the country was to travel by road from Texas by way of Interstate 45 through 75 and back through the Rocky Mountain States. We rented an 8-seater van for the trip and packed necessities for two weeks. That night we prayed and asked God for guidance and protection on the road and in our hotels.

The 7 Steps to A Successful Marriage

The journey took us from the plans of Texas to the midwestern states and into the Deep South before we returned to Texas. We drove leisurely, stopping at cities and points of interest to see interesting sites. We had a blast! It was one of the most outstanding fun things I have done with my family. We all accomplished our goals successfully. My wife and I saw the country; my kids saw the country and had fun. My mother in-law had fun and a story to tell. We set the goal of traveling around the USA knowing that God desires for our families to be happy.

Success may come from accomplishing the goals we set for ourselves, but true success comes from accomplishing the goals that God has set for us. Success is a relative word but real success is only measurable by the person who set the goal.

The word "successful" means, "Resulting in success; assuring success; promoting success; accomplishing what was proposed; having the desired effect; hence, prosperous; fortunate; happy. (Webster). Success in marriage is measured by how much we accomplish for the kingdom of God.

Please understand that this book is "The 7 Steps to A Successful Marriage." These 7 Steps are to be taken one after the other from the first step on the stairway to the last step on the stairway. This book is not "the 7 Secrets", or "the 7 keys" or "the 7 principles" to a successful marriage. We believe that marriage is a lifestyle that requires practical but methodical application of the 7 steps. Secrets, keys and principles of successful marriage involve theories and revelations of what makes marriage work but these steps set out a road map to success in marriage.

A road map tells you how to get to your destination but a General Positioning System (GPS) will show you how to get there. It will tell you when to turn and when to keep straight. *The 7 Steps to A Successful Marriage* is more like a GPS than a road map.

Chapter 1

Lay The Right Foundation

Ask yourself, "What kind of Marriage do I want?"

The foundation of every building is the most important part of the building. It may not be the most visible or the most beautiful part of the building but it is the base that carries the whole building. If the foundation is deep and solid the building will be stable and secured against the floods, hurricanes and storms of life. On the other hand if the foundation is shallow and shaky, the building cannot withstand heavy flooding and the other storms of life. With this knowledge at the back of their minds the best builders seek for the best soil and brick to anchor their building.

When John J. Raskob and Alfred E. Smith were thinking of building the Empire State building they searched for a suitable soil in the New York area. They knew that the tallest building in the world will have to be built on the best foundation in the world. After searching for a good while they chose a site that had enough bedrock on the ground to handle the pressure and burden of carrying a building of that size. Bedrock was the most stable soil available at that time and the most suitable for a building of that size and fame.

The next thing in the process of building the Empire State building was to start the actual construction, but before the construction could start, the site of the building had to be excavated to remove soft soil, debris and to make room for the right soil. Next, the builders dug deep into the earth up to 55 feet (17m) to anchor the world's tallest building. The architects knew that the depth of the foundation had to be proportionate (not directly) to the height of the building. They had to follow a mathematical calculation designed for a building of that magnitude.

The builders also knew that it is not enough to choose the right site for the foundation; they had to build according to the building codes of the City and State for skyscrapers. All these strict rules and codes suggest to us that the foundation of any building is as important as the roof that covers the shell. Most of the time, it is more important than any other part of the building.

After the 1992 Hurricane that devastated South Florida and decimated everything on site, one house remained standing, still firmly anchored to its foundation. A reporter covering the Hurricane asked the owner of the building that was still standing why his house survived the storm, he replied, "I built this house myself. I also built it according to the Florida State building code. I was told that a house built according to code could withstand any hurricane—and it did!" Building according to the divine code for marriage will help your marriage withstand Hurricanes and other elements.

The 7 Steps to A Successful Marriage

Like the Empire State building, your marriage is the tallest building in your life other than your relationship with God. Understand this; if you miss it in marriage, you have missed it in life. As I stated earlier, if you are not saved you live in hell when you die; if you marry the wrong person, you live in hell here in your house; but if you are not saved and marry the wrong person, you are doomed here on earth and after life. Knowing the significance of your marriage you must choose a soil that will withstand all the storms of life; the most stable soil is *the Word*.

Jesus Christ is the most stable soil ever and there is no other soil other than Him. A successful marriage is a marriage that is built on the solid foundation of Jesus Christ and according to the requirements of Jesus Christ. For no other foundation can anyone lay, than that which is laid, which is Christ Jesus. (1 Cor. 3:11) The psalmist noted that, "Unless the LORD builds the house, They labor in vain who build it; Unless the LORD guards the city, The watchman keeps awake in vain" (Psalm 127:1) Marriages are defined by the foundation on which they are established. The foundation you choose to build for your marriage will determine the kind of marriage you build. Today we have all kinds of marriages and I suspect that more options for marriage will evolve in the future.

Recently the lawmakers in Mexico City proposed a bill providing for a two-year marriage trial period for newly wed couples before the marriage becomes permanent. Under the bill such marriages will be optional and expires at the end the two-year trial period unless the couple renewed it. The big reason behind such drastic deviation from the sacred sanctity of marriage was to save the cost and expense of divorce in Mexico City. Recall that Moses permitted the children of Israel to divorce their wives for any reason as a way of easing the stress of marriage. History tells us that any time we have tried to simplify marriage, it backfires on us.

After you have decided on the site of the foundation of your marriage; you have to decide how deep you want to dig for your marriage. In other to choose the site you had to know the site and differentiate that site from all other sites available. Now you need to dig deep because the height of your building has to be proportionate (not directly) to the depth of your foundation. You dig into the foundation of Jesus Christ by digging into His word. He said, "My sheep, hear My voice, and I know them, and they follow Me." (John 10:27)

How can you know His voice if you don't know what His voice sounds like; and how can you know it if you are not following Him (sheepishly) like a sheep. You have to study the bible to find out the building code for your marriage. Paul said "Be diligent to present yourself approved to God, a worker who does not need to be ashamed, rightly dividing the word of truth." (2 Timothy 2:15) Knowledge is power. You have to pray to stay connected with the Maker of marriage. You need all the strength that you can get from Him. Let the love of God guide your actions on how you relate with your spouse and others.

Regrettably, many of us have chosen to build our marriage on a porous site. Some chose Jesus Christ, but they have not dug deep enough to stabilize their marriage. They profess Jesus Christ but they confess the world as their foundation. If your foundation is in Christ, there is no room for divorce and separation. There is only one room and that's for a lifetime relationship. They are not like the sheep that follows Him (sheepishly); instead they say they are His sheep but they follow the voice of the government, the culture, the people and sometimes the devil.

Different Kinds of Foundations

Some of the unstable kinds of foundation sites that we build our marriages on are.

1. Marriage according to our mothers and fathers

This marriage is characterized by selfishness that does not accommodate the other parties in the union. This type of marriage is against God's plan because the man is expected to leave his father and mother behind and create a new life, his own life and destiny. When you do marriage just the way your father and mother did it you carry the rituals of your mother and the traditions of your father into your new home.

2. Marriage according to the Government

This kind of marriage is always changing because politicians and lawmaker define marriage based on what will get them the most votes during election. In this type of marriage, God does not rule, the majority of the people rule and the government back them up with the protection of the court. Under this marriage anybody can play any role depending on the circumstance. It makes it easy to start your marriage relationship and easier to terminate the marriage. There is no oneness in the marriage because you are expected to keep your individuality even in if you live in a community state. Whatever you had before the marriage is separate and apart from the marriage. Whatever you inherit from your parents is separate and apart from the marriage. If you win lotto or receive a settlement because of bodily injury, it does not belong to the union. The marriage is only concerned with the period of the marriage. In this marriage, you can get in at any time and get out any time you desire. This is against God's plan because the two remain two.

3. Marriage according to cultural/tradition

This type of marriage is based on the cultures and traditions of men. Each culture and tradition has its own rules and regulations. Some permit polygamy; some permit men to keep girlfriends, men dominate some, while women dominate some. While most marriages based on culture are expected to last for lifetime, they rarely fulfill the purpose of marriage.

4. Marriage according to Hollywood

This is the kind of marriage promoted by Hollywood stars and Reality stars. In Hollywood the rule of marriages is "If we are not happy, we call it quits". Marriage according to Hollywood is for convenience and sometimes for monetary gain. Some people have been known to enter into a marriage arrangement in other to gain free publicity and resurrect their career.

5. Marriage according to the trends in the Society

This kind of marriage promotes the thought that "You don't need to be married to enjoy the benefits of marriage." You can live like you are married even though you are not married. Marriage according to the society is always evolving. Sometimes it is between a man and a woman, sometimes it is between a man and man or a woman and another woman. You can act like you are married for as long as you like. These days the society does not seem to care as long as you are monogamous while you are in it. Cohabitation is accepted in the society now as a kind of marriage that demands our sympathy.

6. Marriage according to religion

Marriage according to the church means you attended premarital counseling, had your wedding according to the rules of the church and you have not had any divorce. The church considers you married until you get a divorced. The church is not always concerned about how you do marriage but that you stay married. It is common to see dead marriages walking in the Church. Sometimes the dead marriages sit in the front row too, sing in the choir, preach the sermon and even conduct wedding ceremonies. The Church believes that success in marriage is measured by how long the marriage lasts without divorce and separation. You just have to stay in marriage to get the blessings of marriage. If you leave, it's a sin. If you stay, it's a success.

Choose the Right Foundation for your Marriage

A successful marriage has to be built on a solid foundation of the word of God. We must see marriage as God sees marriage in order to do marriage as God intended for marriage to be done. He has provided instructions on:

1. What marriage means

2. Who we should marry and who we should not to marry

3. Who is qualified for marriage and who is not qualified

4. The duration of marriage

5. The role of the parties in a marriage

6. The role of other people in our marriage.

Success in marriage comes from reading the instructions for marriage and applying it in our own marriage. From our choice of spouse to the way we do marriage, God has predetermined everything. Following the manual is for our own good and ignoring the manual is bad for us. The first marriage established by God failed because Adam and Eve did not follow the instructions. Furthermore, God deserves a central role in our marriage and home. He made us in His image for us to give Him praise and fellowship with Him. The first couple fellowshipped with God on daily bases so much that they even "…heard the sound of the LORD God walking in the garden in the cool of the day" Genesis 3:8a. God still demands the same fellowship from us today. When we give God the first place in our marriage, our marriage becomes the first thing in His face.

Beloved, the first step to maintaining that foundation is to connect with the Maker of marriage and stay connected with Him. Some of us keep our God in our closet for late night prayers. Some remember God only at the dinner table for blessing our meal while others remember God only in time of trouble. The reality is that you cannot build a successful marriage without building a vibrant family altar.

The second step to maintain that foundation is ensure that the family altar remains active with spiritual activities. After all your marriage and home is the first church that you and your children go to before going to the church in the street.

"For I have known him, in order that he may command his children and his household after him, that they keep the way of the Lord, to do righteousness and justice, that the Lord may bring to Abraham what He has spoken to him." (Genesis 18:19)

"You shall teach them diligently to your children, and shall talk of them when you sit in your house, when you walk by the way, when you lie down, and when you rise up." (Deuteronomy 6:7)

"And you, fathers, do not provoke your children to wrath, but bring them up in the training and admonition of the Lord." (Ephesians 6:4.)

How to lay the Right Foundation?

The acquisition of wisdom is the prerequisite for establishing a successful marriage and for building a stable home. "Wisdom is the principal thing; therefore get wisdom: and with all your getting get understanding." (Proverbs 4:7) This statement is perhaps more relevant to marriage than any other undertaking.

"The wise woman builds her house, but with her own hands the foolish one tears hers down". Proverbs 14:1

"Through wisdom a house is built, and by understanding it is established, by knowledge the rooms are filled with all precious and pleasant riches" (Proverbs 24:3, 4)

The virtuous woman of Proverbs 31:10-31 was praised for the wise choices she made. Her decisions added extraordinary values to her husband and her household. Wisdom is therefore the foundational step to a successful marriage and the lack of wisdom leads to gross failures in marriage.

She opens her mouth with wisdom, and on her tongue is the law of kindness. She watches over the ways of her household, and does not eat the bread of idleness. Her children rise up and call her blessed; Her husband also, and he praises her: "Many daughters have done well, but you excel them all." Charm is deceitful and beauty is passing, but a woman who fears the Lord, she shall be praised. Give her of the fruit of her hands, and let her own works praise her in the gates. (Proverbs 31:26-31)

Now the wisdom for a successful marriage is the wisdom that comes from God the Maker of marriage. This kind of wisdom is defined as knowledge guided by understanding. "Understanding" means knowing things in their right relationship or order. It is not the wisdom we receive from school or from reading books but the wisdom that comes from the fear of God because the fear of God is the beginning of wisdom.

The absence of the fear of God is the primary reason for the high rate of divorce and dysfunctional families. Otherwise why would anybody get married three, four or five times in his or her lifetime? If you truly love God, fear and reverence God, why would you file and prosecute two, three and up to five divorce petitions in your life time knowing that God hates divorce. He said what God has joined together, let no man separate. Now I have heard some people argue that their first marriage was not joined together by God therefore their divorce should not make God mad and to that I say, "This is not funny!"

Many of us are now so desperate that we are willing to try out marriage for a short while. We are willing to enter into a marriage relationship knowing that it has no chance of surviving beyond the first few years. We just want to enjoy it for the moment. The various attempts to redefine marriage according to Hollywood, the government, our cultures and traditions are evidence of the state of marriage. Such experiments as the one in Mexico City, is bound to create more problems for the communities.

The marriage of Adam and Eve which was the first marriage established by God failed as soon as it was established because Adam and Eve were outwitted by the Serpent. "Now the Serpent was more cunning than any beast of the field which the Lord has made." Genesis 3:1. God gave the first couple everything they needed to enjoy their union in the Garden of Eden including instruction on how to be successful as husband and wife such as:

1. Be fruitful and multiple, fill the earth and subdue it, have dominion over the fish of the sea, over the bird of the air, and over every living thing that moves on the earth. Genesis 1:28

2. Tend and keep the garden of Eden

3. Eat every tree of the garden except the tree of knowledge of good and evil. If you eat the tree if good and evil you shall surely die. Genesis 2:16-17.

4. Leave your father and mother and be joined to your wife and become one flesh. Genesis 2:24.

Adam and Eve choose to obey the serpent and disobeyed God. That was the end of the first marriage and the beginning of the problems of marriage. From that point on Adam and Eve lost their destiny of dominion and their position as the manager of God's estate even though they stayed together as husband and wife. Notice that before they disobeyed God, and followed the serpent's advice, Adam and Eve lived their life according to the manual. Their marriage was a blessing and not a burden to themselves and to the Kingdom of God. Contrast that with their life after the disobedience. They were sent out of the Garden of Eden, they had to work hard (actually toil) for their living, Eve's name was changed from "woman" which means "because she was taking out of man" to "Eve" which means, "the mother of all living things". Same thing happens when we bet against the principles of God.

When people read the account of the temptation of Eve and the fall of Adam, they frequently skip over where Adam changed Eve's name from "Woman" to "Eve". Unfortunately, fewer things are more significant to the marriage than Adam renaming his wife "the mother of all living thing." Essentially "woman" went from being known by her content and connection with God, (her most distinguished title and the only creation of God that shared authority, power and privilege with Adam) to her role in the new world.

Yes they lost God's favor and their position of dominion. Yet Adam and Eve remained husband and wife for the most part until Adam renamed his wife Eve. Naming someone or something is a very significant event. A name is not just for getting our attention but a name gives life and transforms life too. We create the kind of person we desire by the name we give that person. Ultimately we all become what we call ourselves or in practical terms what we answer to. Naming and names are very powerful.

Adam had the exclusive power to name everything that God created including his wife Eve. We also have the power to name our spouse and our marriage. As long as we are connected with God we can define and redefine our marriage by what we say or don't say. "A man's stomach shall be satisfied from the fruit of his mouth; from the produce of his lips he shall be filled. Death and life are in the power of the tongue, and those who love it will eat its fruits" (Proverbs 18:20-21). Yes, you can make and remake your marriage no matter how bad it has been so far.

Many of us choose the wrong foundation for our marriage. We build our marriage on the most expensive fittings and paint. We decorate it with the most exquisite and expensive paintings and furniture. Then we host expensive weddings and invite the crème de la crème of the society hoping that the marriage survives but knowing that the odds are stacked up against us.

At the beginning everything looks good, that is until the first storm hits; the painting immediately scales, the fittings come loose and the furniture are soaked with water and ruined. Then we bail out because the house built on a faulty foundation is ruined. The truth is that the house did not stand a chance! The psalmist asked "If the foundation be destroyed, what can the righteous (or anybody for that matter) do?" (Psalm 11:3)

The irony is that the same newspapers, radio stations and television houses that celebrated the wedding are there to cremate the marriage and sing its funeral songs. The good thing is there is hope for the fallen house and the messed up marriage. The angels will celebrate your victory this time around.

Chapter 2

Marry For The Right Purpose

Ask yourself, "Why do I want to be married?"

The second step to a successful marriage is to decide why you want to get married. If you are already married your second step is to review why you got married. I realize that quiet a number of people got married because they found someone they love and decided to spend the rest of their life with the person. These are the soul mate seekers who believe that finding their soul mate is the answer to all their questions about marriage. If you are one of those in this group, good for you for marrying for love and love alone. Adam appears to have married for this reason also when he chose Eve.

Nonetheless choosing your life partner is the most important choice you will make in your lifetime other than choosing to serve God. In Genesis 24:7 we see the story of Rebecca and Isaac. The bible says that Abraham that sent his servant to choose a wife for his son Isaac. Before sending the

The 7 Steps to A Successful Marriage

servant on his way Abraham prayed for God to help his servant in the task of finding a wife for his son. "The Lord God of heaven, who took me from my father's house and from the land of my family, and who spoke to me and swore to me saying, "To your descendants I will give this land', He will send His angel before you and shall take a wife for my son from there." From this we know that Rebecca was a product of prayers but the story did not tell us why Rebecca agreed to marry Isaac who she had not seen.

If you got married according to the rules of the impostors like Hollywood, Government, Society or Culture, then the purpose of your marriage may be pursing the agenda of the impostor. For instance, if you got married according to the rules of Hollywood, your purpose for getting married may be convenience, companionship or career. In Hollywood whenever those factors are not in the marriage the parties are free to terminate the marriage. That is why marriages in Hollywood are full of pomp and pageantry but hardly outlasts the ovation.

Recently, the reality star Kim Kardashian was married, separated, and filed for divorce from her husband within 72 days of the exchange of vows. The wedding itself was one of the most expensive weddings in the history of Hollywood. Do you know her reason for filling the divorce? Well you guessed it right "I am not happy in this marriage and If I am not happy…, I can't be where I am not happy" That is the rule in Hollywood. They rationalize the breakup of their marriage with statements like "Why stay when you are not happy?"

Not being happy is not a good reason to terminate a marriage in the eyes of God. If we all get a divorce because we are not happy, no one will be married. The reality is that in marriage, there are times when we are not happy and there are many times when we are very happy.

If on the other hand you decided to get married according to God's principle, then your purpose has to align with God's purpose for establishing marriage. Yes, your marriage is not for fun alone. God is always generous but never frivolous. Everything that He created He created for a reason and for a role in the Kingdom. Likewise, God, the maker of marriage has a definite purpose for establishing marriage. Accordingly, the success of a particular marriage is not necessarily measured by the longevity of the marriage, but by how much of its original purpose the marriage accomplished or is pursuing.

What if you were asked to write down what success in your marriage means to you? I bet we will get a different meaning of successful marriage from each married person here because each one of us has his or her own meaning of success. However it is important for each couple to have a well-defined purpose. Knowing where you are going makes your journey easier and adds a matrix to it. The vision of the union must be clear and visible for the couple and everyone around them to see. A successful marriage is a marriage that fulfills God's purpose for marriage.

Please understand that marriage intertwines the two destinies and purposes into one destiny and purpose. I remember a question that was posed to us during a couples' banquet in December of 2009. The Lady said she was called to be an evangelist and was working in the mission field overseas when her husband met her. Her husband is called into pastoral ministry, pastoring a church. This sister does not feel fulfilled working as a pastor's wife. She feels guilty for abandoning her passion for winning souls and planting churches as a missionary. Her question was whether she was wrong to ask her husband to release her to go do her mission work.

Let's not get too emotional over these issues. Let us look at what the bible says before we follow our passion. Eve was created as a helper fit for Adam. If Eve had decided to leave the Garden of Eden, how much of help would she have been to her husband? Secondly, Adam and Eve were given the same assignment, the same instructions, and the same blessings. They suffered the same fate when their marriage failed and lost their position of dominion jointly.

Can you imagine what will happen if two people who are supposed to travel from Texas to Florida by road had two different destinations and routs in mind? One thinks they are travelling from Texas to California by road, while the other believes they are both travelling from Texas to Florida by air? I can imagine it because I see it happen all the time. First the couple cannot get to their intended destinations at the same time. Second they will not get there together. One will get there in three hours while the other gets there in 24 hours. No wonder some want divorce while others want to stay married.

Not having the same purpose makes husband think his marriage is over while the wife thinks marriage is for a lifetime; or wife thinks marriage is only when she is happy, while husband thinks marriage is for better and for worse.

What then is the purpose of marriage? The primary purpose of marriage is for man and woman to live in dominion and seek the kingdom of God. The bible says,

"Then God blessed them, and God said to them, "Be fruitful and multiply; fill the earth and subdue it; have dominion over the fish of the sea, over the birds of the air, and over every living thing that moves on the earth."(Genesis 1:28)

Marriage was therefore established to fulfill God's purpose in three ways:

1. **Marriage is for Destiny:** The destinies of every married couple are intertwined together forever. Their combined effort gives them a better chance of fulfilling their destiny. "Therefore a man shall leave his father and mother and be joined to his wife, and they shall become one flesh. So then, they are no longer two but one flesh. Therefore what God has joined together let not man separate". Mathew 19:5-6. Marriage unites your destiny with your spouse's destiny and you are no longer separable even if you desire to do so. This is the primary reason for God's attitude toward divorce. Divorce attempts to separate what God has joined together. Success in marriage starts from understanding its significance in life and committing to sticking with it through the ups and downs.

Some are now teaching that marriage is a spiritual event that ends with the spiritual death of either of the parties. Nothing is further from the truth and certainly more misleading to all those looking for a way out of their marriage. Marriage is designed to be a once in a lifetime event. Instead of looking for a way out, look for a way to stay in your marriage and enjoy it.

2. **Marriage is for Companionship:** It is written that "It is not good for man to be alone; I will make him a helper comparable to him." (Genesis 2:18) Marriage provides emotional, sexual, intellectual and spiritual companionship to the couple. "Live joyfully with the wife whom you love all the days of your vain life which He has given you under the sun, all your days of vanity; for that is your portion in life, and in the labor which you perform under the sun." Ecclesiastes 9:9

The 7 Steps to A Successful Marriage

As you can see from these scriptures, marriage provides companionship for the couple. This was so important to God that newlywed couples in Israel are exempt from war for one whole year to enable them enjoy themselves. "If a man has recently married, he must not be sent to war or have any other duty laid on him. For one year he is to be free to stay at home and bring happiness to the wife he has married" Deuteronomy 24:5. If your purpose in marriage does not include being a good companion to your spouse, you are not following the maker's manual. Couples must make time for each other for the sake of their marriage.

Please understand that there is no other way for us to satisfy our sexual needs other than through marriage. Marriage is exclusive between a man and his wife and that relationship is for life. A couple is not permitted to seek sexual satisfaction from any other person or any other source as long as both of them are alive. That is why pornography is as bad as actual intercourse.

Notice how the scripture put it in Proverbs 5:18-21;

"Drink water from your own cistern,

Running water from your own well.

Should your springs overflow in the streets,

Your streams of water in the public squares?

Let them be yours alone,

Never to be shared with strangers.

The 7 Steps to A Successful Marriage

May your fountain be blessed,

And may you rejoice in the wife of your youth.

A loving doe, a graceful deer—

May her breasts satisfy you always,

May you ever be captivated by her love.

Why be captivated, my son, by an adulteress?

Why embrace the bosom of another man's wife?

For a man's ways are in full view of the LORD,

And he examines all his paths.

The evil deeds of a wicked man ensnare him;

The cords of his sin hold him fast.

He will die for lack of discipline,

Led astray by his own great folly".

3. **Marriage is for Covenant:** The Marriage relationship is a covenant relationship and not a contractual relationship. Pastor Jack Hayford described covenant marriage as follows: "The covenant of marriage is the single most important human bond that holds all of God's work on the planet together. It is no small wonder that the Lord is passionate about the sanctity of marriage and the stability of the home. This covenant of marriage is based on the covenant God has made with us. It is in the power of His promise to her mankind that our personal covenant of marriage can be kept against the forces that would destroy homes and ruin lives." (Hayford, J. W. The Spirit-

The 7 Steps to A Successful Marriage

Filled Family: Holy Wisdom to Build Happy Homes. Nashville: Thomas Nelson). A Covenant carries a higher and deeper commitment than a contract or a mere promise.

In the time of old covenants were sealed with the "shading" of blood. The shading of blood comes either at the end of the agreement or at the end but never at the middle of the negotiation. This includes covenants between God and man; and covenants made by men and women. Covenant made without the shading of blood do not carry hefty punishment for its violation. The marriage covenant is not exempt from this shading of blood even though the blood that is shed in the marriage covenant is not red blood, it is blood nonetheless. The sexual relationship between a man and his wife is the celebration of that seal of the marriage covenant.

Sexual intercourse was a means of sealing the covenant of marriage with the mixing of the blood of the husband and the wife. God's intention is for husband and wife to be one and be joined together. He expects this union to remain so sacred and so exclusive, that it must not be desecrated by anyone.

I know that some may be reading this book and wondering where they fit in with the covenant and destiny part of marriage because they have had prior marriages or engaged in prior sexual relationship outside marriage or even entered into marriage without knowing all these implications. Well if you have engaged in sexual intercourse with someone who is not your spouse, the sin is always condemned but you are not condemned. How many of us haven't in this promiscuous world? Sex is so prevalent that it's now harder to be in the world and not be of the world. Thank God for the blood of Jesus that cleanses us from all sins. As long as you have asked for forgiveness, the blood makes all things new for you.

The 7 Steps to A Successful Marriage

"Therefore, if anyone is in Christ, he is a new creation; old things have passed away; behold, all things have become new" (2 Corinthians 5:17) The scriptures says, "There is therefore now no condemnation to those who are in Christ Jesus, who do not walk according to the flesh, but according to the Spirit" (Romans 8:1) If the son has set you free, you are free indeed.

Note that a marriage can only become a success when the parties aligned their individual purpose with God's purpose for your marriage. In marriage when we seek first the kingdom of God, He adds the rest to us for our enjoyment. Too often we pursue the "rest' and leave the "first". Some of the rest that we pursue are:

1. To have Children,
2. To have a spouse like others
3. To wear a ring on my fingers like other women
4. To "shame the devil and my enemies"
5. For sexual satisfaction
6. To compensate him/her for all that he/she did for me etc.

These are noble ideas but they are only the fringe benefits of marriage and not the main benefit of marriage. If you want a successful marriage, follow the maker's manual for marriage from the beginning to the end of marriage and your marriage will be successful. Please understand that your marriage need not be successful in the eyes of the world but only successful before God. In fact most successful marriages are graded poorly by the world. You will be surprised at all the wrong reasons people go into marriage.

Why did I get married?

The 7 Steps to A Successful Marriage

An old man was called to propose a toast for his friend who was retiring after many years of service. The retiring man was a recluse who only associated with this old man while he was in the office. When it was time for the toast, the old man got up and said "Well, Mr. Oliphant was born when his buddies were born. He went to school when everybody else did and graduated when the time came for graduation. When they were getting a job, he got a job as well and as you all know; he did his job here just as most of us do our job. And now he is retiring at the age of retirement". The room exploded with a thunderous ovation. What the people did not know was the old man did not know anything about the retiring man other than what everybody else knew. Yes they had lunch everyday but all they talked about was gambling and women. So the old did not know what to say. Pretty impressive accomplishment you might say; but some of us are like that.

- We got married because our mates were getting married.
- We do marriage just as our parents did marriage;
- We end marriage for the same reason that people get divorce.

He who does not know where he is going, any road will lead him there. Marriage is therefore for companionship. Marriage is the union of one man and one woman. Marriage is God's platform for building His kingdom. You are a part of the greater kingdom of God and your marriage is crucial to the master plan of God. For your marriage to be successful, you and your spouse must share the same vision and see that vision from the same platform.

Chapter 3

Choose The Right Partner

Ask yourself "What kind of person do I want to marry?"

Ladies please understand that you are not commanded to marry any man. You required to respect and reverence the man you choose to marry. Gentlemen, you are required to marry someone who you love enough to lay down your life for. How often people marry the wrong person because they feel obligated to that person. A man marries a woman because she is pregnant for him, or she has invested so much on him, his family says so. When a woman marries a boy she very well knows she will never respect or submit to for whatever reason she sets herself up for failure and unhappiness.

The third step to a successful marriage is to choose the right person and be the right person for your spouse. No other step in the process of building a successful marriage has more practical applications than marrying or choosing the right person. If you got married for the wrong reasons, you can change your mind later and return to follow God's instructions. If you get married with the assumption that marriage is according to whatever reason, you can always change your purpose.

However if you marry the wrong person you are stuck with that person. The only saving grace is for the wrong person to become the right person by converting to your belief. Time and time again the bible warns us against marrying certain kinds of people. The bible is full of stories of people who married the wrong person and the consequences they suffered. Genesis 24:3-4; 28:1-2, 24:3-4, Deuteronomy 7:3, Joshua 23:12.

If the best reason for marriage is to pursue your destiny in life, then the worse thing is not fulfilling your destiny in life. Choosing the wrong person is the surest way to guarantee failure in marriage. In the same way, marrying the right person gives us a head start in the journey of life. Adam saw his wife and exclaimed "This is now bone of my bone and the flesh of my flesh; She shall be called Woman, because she was taken out of man". (Genesis 2:23) Finding that piece of you can mean the difference between success and failure in life. I pray for all those searching for the right person. There is nothing more exhilarating than finding your soul mate.

It happened for me in the fall of 1983, my sophomore year in college. I was on the hallway of one the class rooms waiting for a meeting to start when I looked across the lawn about 50 yards away and saw this beautiful lady wearing a pink striped dress with her hair all made up and walking with a stride that was musical. It happened that she was coming to the same meeting I was waiting to start. She was new in college and we were introduced to each other later that evening and from that day we become acquaintances, then friends, then close friends and ended up married. When you find your "wife" or "husband", the feeling is unbelievable and the chemistry is automatic and unprecedented.

Choosing God's choice is for your own good and for the smooth operation of the complex institution of marriage. Some of the benefits of choosing someone that shares your faith and belief are:

1. It helps fulfill God's original plan for creating man, which is to make man a 'little Gods' that will be fruitful and multiply by reproducing more little "Gods". If we marry someone that does not share our belief, we corrupt the purity of the bloodline. Malachi 2:15
2. It is not only important that we look like God, it is equally important that we act like Him in all we do. God demands that we teach our children His ways. "And these words that I command you today shall be on your heart. You shall teach them diligently to your children, and shall talk of them when you sit in your house, and when you walk by the way, and when you lie down, and when you rise. You shall bind them as a sign on your hand, and they shall be as frontlets between your eyes. You shall write them on the doorposts of your house and on your gates". Deuteronomy 7:6-7. Marriage and family is the only platform to accomplish that purpose Psalm 82:6, Psalm 8:5-6
3. Marrying someone who does not believe in God or someone who believes in God but does not have the same passion, love and enthusiasm for the things of God is likely to draw you away from God. This is not my theory but God's instructions. "You shall make no

covenant with them and show no mercy to them. You shall not intermarry with them, giving your daughters to their sons or taking their daughters for your sons, for they would turn away your sons from following me, to serve other gods. Then the anger of the LORD would be kindled against you, and he would destroy you quickly. Deuteronomy 7:3-4. (ESV)
4. Marriage has its benefits but some of those benefits are available only to those who believe in God. One of the benefits of being married is the power of agreement. God is present wherever (and now whenever) two or three are present. Marriage gives you 24 hours of access to the presence of God. Two cannot work together except they agree. Amos 3:3. If you cannot agree on who created you, you are not likely to agree on anything spiritually. Spiritual agreement is more important than physical agreement because everything we do is controlled in the spiritual realm.

The first person that violated this rule was Esau, the son of Isaac. The bible says that "When Esau was forty years old, he took Judith the daughter of Beeri the Hittite to be his wife, and Basemath the daughter of Elon the Hittite, and they made life bitter for Isaac and Rebekah" Genesis 26:34-35. Look at what Paul said about entering into a relationship with people who do not share your belief,

"Do not be yoked together with unbelievers. For what do righteousness and wickedness have in common? Or what fellowship can light have with darkness? What harmony is there between Christ and Belial? What does a believer have in common with an unbeliever? What agreement is there between the temple of God and idols? For we are the temple of the living God. As God has said: "I will live with them and walk among them, and I will be their God, and they will be my people" 2 Corinthians 6:14-16

Marriage is one thing that the bible did not just tell us what to do but it also shows us how it's done. The success of our marriage depends on our ability to choose the right partner. One of the worse things that can happen to anybody is to travel on this life journey with the wrong person. It is important to carefully and prayerfully find your driving buddy in this journey of life.

Fortunately for us God did not just tell us who to marry; He also gave guideline to make the right choice. One of the guidelines is found in Genesis 2:24 which says, "For this reason a man shall leave his father and mother and be joined to his wife and they shall become one flesh". A "man" means a fully-grown man that is matured enough and qualified to marry. This requirement is critical to the success of marriage because of the responsibilities that the man will assume in marriage.

Notice also that God was specific as to what He wanted to do when it came to creating a woman for Adam. It was not just any woman but a helper comparable to him. "It is not good that man should be alone, I will make him a helper comparable to him" Genesis 2:18.

Now if after knowing these instructions a woman decides to marry a boy instead of a man she will suffer the consequences. Note, just being of age does not qualify a man for marry without the requisite maturity that is need to handle the complex emotions of a woman. He must be a man in deed and able to stand on his own.

The 7 Steps to A Successful Marriage

I know a young lady that got married three years ago. The man is in his mid-30s, gainfully employed and had lived on his own for many years. Right from the beginning while they were courting, it was obvious to the lady that his mother was unduly influencing him. The young lady thought about cancelling the wedding plans but decided against it, hoping for the best. Well, three years and two kids later, the couple is in the family court seeking to end the marriage. The man could not free himself from the shackles of his mother's grip. Every decision had to be run through the mother and his wife's opinion did not matter in the house. That is an example of a man who is not qualified for marriage.

Additionally, the man leaving his mother and father must be joined to his wife and not just any other woman. Please understand that your marriage is comprised of three persons: God, Husband and Wife. Genesis 2:18, Ecclesiastes 4:8-12. Fortunately for us, our God has given us sufficient road maps to find our marriage partner. Deuteronomy 7:1-6.

The 7 Steps to A Successful Marriage

Chapter 4
Know Your Role In Marriage

Ask yourself, "What is My Role in My Marriage?"

God's Order and Hierarchy

Your family is the smallest unit of the church of God. It is God's "A" team for the work of the Kingdom. It is therefore important to God for husband and wife to work in harmony. To realize this goal, God has set the affairs of marriage and His kingdom in order and in a hierarchy of authority. "However, I want you to realize that Christ has authority over every man, a husband has authority over his wife, and God has authority over Christ". (1 Corinthians 11:3 GOD'S WORD)

Can you imagine what will happen if Jesus Christ wakes up one day and challenges God; or if a man wakes up one morning and claims to be Jesus Christ? Some have actually done it. The last time there was a meaningful challenge to the authority of God we had chaos in the Kingdom and massive realignments in heaven. Lucifer the archangel assigned to guard heaven lost his job and his position for declaring himself equal to God. The same thing could happen to anyone that upsets this order of things in his/her marriage. You may not lose your position in heaven; but you will certainly lose your position in your marriage. Please understand that when a man abdicates his responsibility as a husband or father; or a wife takes over her husband's position, their marriage suffers and we have a dysfunctional family.

Efficiency of the Union

In marriage the husband and wife are assigned specific roles to avoid conflict and also to increase efficiency. Whatever one spouse cannot do has to be done jointly. For instance in child bearing, the man brings his seed; the woman brings her egg before a child could be conceived. Even the roles that a man can do alone, the woman can complement him to do it better and with ease. That is the principles of teamwork at its best. It is critical that we understand why God set things up the way He set it up and our role in the big picture of the Kingdom of God.

For a team to be efficient and unstoppable, each team member has to know his or her role; accept that role and aspire to play that role better than any other member of the team and better than the opposition. Furthermore each member has to know enough of the other members role and be ready to pay a little bit of it should the need arise. This is true of marriage and families too. Any couple or team able to achieve this level of efficiency is unstoppable!!!

Notice what Ecclesiastes says about teamwork and invariably marriage.

"Two people are better than one because [together]

They have a good reward for their hard work.

If one falls, the other can help his friend get up.

But how tragic it is for the one who is [all] alone when he falls.

There is no one to help him get up.

Again, if two people lie down together,

They can keep warm, but how can one person keep warm?

Though another may overpower one person,

Two people can resist one opponent.

A triple-braided rope is not easily broken"

(Ecclesiastes 4:9-12 GOD'S WORD)

Did you notice that at the end of the scripture the discussion changed from t "two" to talking about three - "A triple-braided rope is not easily broken"? Two is the number that guarantees the presence of God but it is not every two that guarantees the presence of God. It is only the two that "agree" that can usher in the presence of God. Knowing your role and playing it without murmuring or complaining is a prerequisite to the success of your marriage.

Insurance and Continuity

Working as team does not only guarantee better reward for your labor, it also ensures continuation of the union. The scripture we quoted above says "But how tragic it is for the one who is [all] alone when he falls. There is no one to help him get up".

I remember a story that illustrates this point even better. There was this couple who got married in the early 1980's while in college. They graduated from the college soon afterward they got marriage. The husband who is an engineer got a lucrative job with a major electronic company almost immediately after his graduation. His salary and benefits from the Fortune 500 employee was enviable. He quickly distanced himself from the wife, maintained his own bank account and only paid the house bills. He never took the wife on his numerous trips around the world and never gave her allowance. About the same time his wife got a job with the state government. Needless to say that her salary and benefits were nothing compared to what her husband earned.

This situation continued for several years until the wife decided to go back to school. Two years later she graduated as a registered nurse but stayed in school until she completed her masters' degree in nursing as a Nurse Practitioner. At that time things had turned bad for her husband who lost his job with the Fortune 500 Company and could not get another job. After staying at home for several months he converted one of his personal vehicles to a taxicab and started driving taxi.

Meanwhile his wife opened a medical clinic and was making a lot of money. She remembered all the bad things her husband did to her when he had his lucrative job and treated him the same way. She kept her own financial affairs to herself, paid only the minor bills in the house and took only her three children with her on annual vacations. Three years after graduating from college the wife had a malpractice lawsuit in her clinic, this was followed by a criminal investigation that eventually led to her license as a nurse practitioner being revoked and her clinic closed down. Talk about déjà vu! Now you see why God wants you to work together with your spouse? It is for your own good because two are always better than one.

Unity of the Union

God wants the husband and wife to remain together as a winning team for the kingdom and to reproduce them. As the man cannot carry the unborn baby and the woman has no sperm they must work together to conceive a child. No role is less important than the other but some roles are leadership roles and that office needs to be respected and supported. Submitting to the husband makes for cohesion in the management of the marriage and family. That's why the bible admonishes wives to submit to their own husband and husbands to love their wife. Loving your wife ensures her cooperation and loyalty in the pursuit of your divine mandate. After all God has said that it is not good for you, the husband to be alone. You need help!

On the other hand I can't understand why it's hard for some women to accept the instructions on "Submission". After all you are not submitting to just any man but your own husband, the man you chose by yourself and for yourself. You chose him to be your husband so why can't you trust him? I can appreciate the challenges of submitting to a husband that is failing in his role as the husband or a husband that is not lead by the spirit. Unfortunately a husband is a husband just as a wife is a wife.

Recognition of Strengths and Weaknesses

God recognizes that some members of the marriage union are fragile. That's why husbands are admonished to love their wives as Christ loved the Church. A husband should be ready to die for his wife. The couple may depend on the wife to provide spiritual leadership but only for a short while. God did not give the woman the responsibility of leading the family.

What then are the roles of the Parties in a marriage?

The Role of the Husband

A husband wears both spiritual and secular hats as the leader of the family. In the secular sense he acts as the father, husband, wife; and leader. In the spiritual sense he wears all kinds of hats any time of his life. His role as a father is quite different from his role as husband. As a father he is a teacher, a leader and a provider. As a husband he is the lover and the spiritual head of his wife. His number one obligation to her is to love her but his primary obligation to God as far as the marriage is concerned is to preserve, nurture and present her to God as a saint ready for heaven. It is a huge responsibility. In each role the husband is required to pay the ultimate price and sacrifice for his wife if need be. He is expected to be her ferocious defender and a gentle protector.

> Husbands, love your wives as Christ loved the church and gave his life for it. He did this to make the church holy by cleansing it, washing it using water along with spoken words. Then he could present it to himself as a glorious church, without any kind of stain or wrinkle—holy and without faults. So husbands must love their wives as they love their own bodies. A man who loves his wife loves himself. No one ever hated his own body. Instead, he feeds and takes care of it, as Christ takes care of the church.
>
> Ephesians 5:25-29 GOD'S WORD

The 7 Steps to A Successful Marriage

In his role as a leader, the husband leads his family through the maze of life as they pursue their destiny and fulfill the purpose of marriage. In his role as a breadwinner, he makes tough decisions on how to provide for the family and works hard toward it for the general welfare of the family. These roles are so important that any man who cannot perform these functions is not qualified for marriage. As the head the husband has the following responsibilities:

- The Good Brain that thinks for the family,
- Watchful eyes for observation and protection,
- A mouth to bless and curse,
- Powerful Nose that breaths oxygen (life) and smells (perceive) carbon monoxide.

Unfortunately a lot of men think that providing for their family is the only responsibility they have in the marriage. They work hard all week long and when they come home, it's time to relax and rest. They ignore their role as a leader, as a lover and their responsibility toward their wife. In fact a lot of men are not aware of their responsibility as a Spiritual head of the family. You see this every Sunday morning; women and mothers are in churches with their children while their husbands and the fathers are at home sleeping, watching football or away traveling for their job. That is why the so called successful men make money available to their children, provide housing, food and pay school fees and never show up to provide leadership in the house. They end of raising children ill prepared to manage their wealth.

Regrettably a good number of women accept and sometimes acquiesce to their man's long hours at work, two jobs and many days on the road travelling without them. As long as he is bringing home the money, she steps up to the plate and becomes mom and dad. She runs the house, the school runs, the PTA's and suppresses her needs in exchange for the big house, the luxury cars, the jewelries and the good life. She thinks she is happy that money is not a problem but feels empty and worthless. Eventually she starts messing with the other men and before you know it the marriage ends. The marriage actually ended the moment the priorities were misplaced. Money does not provide leadership and material things without people become monotonous.

The reality is that money may not be a problem but the children may be paying a price for that lifestyle. I love the way Anne Romney, the wife of republican candidate for 2012 United States presidential elections put it, "Every family have their problem. Money happens not to be ours" Yes money is not the only problem in marriage.

Time and time again I read about men, and I hear them express regrets with a deep sigh of pain on how they did not spend time with their loved ones especially their children. These are the men who focused all their attention on being a breadwinner but paid no attention to being a leader and a father to their children. A few months ago a man stood up in a class and proudly said "I have four children but I never married their mothers, we were all good like that but I have always paid child support for all my kids. They live with their mothers and I do my thing. I have a girlfriend that I kick it with." When asked what kind of relationship he has with the children, he said "Good! I paid all my child support; I don't owe them anything. I never lived with them or their mother. I think they came out okay."

These are the men who forget that the purpose of having a child is to raise godly offspring for the Kingdom of God and responsible citizens for the society. The purpose of having a child is not to feed them. Child support only provides food for a child; it does not teach the child how to provide food for himself when you stop paying support. It does not teach your boy how to treat a woman, or how to change a tire, make a tie or how to be a man. He is growing to be a man on your child support but he does not know how to be a man. Your boy can't control his sexual rage and emotions. This child has no chance in this competitive world. You set him up for failure by the choices you made.

Your child support does not teach your little girl how to love and handle a man. She never saw you say "I love you" or otherwise express love to her mother so when someone says I love you, she is confused and thinks it's the best thing that happened to anyone in the world. She responds with the best thing she has; her body because that's what she has seen her mama do all her life. She is only seen you argue with her mother over child support, medical insurance and go to court fighting for child support. Your little girl grew up with your child support; but she is not prepared for the life ahead of her.

Here are a few things the bible said about your responsibility to your wife and the children as the husband and the father.

"Husbands, love your wives as Christ loved the church and gave his life for it. He did this to make the church holy by cleansing it, washing it using water along with spoken words. Then he could present it to himself as a glorious church, without any kind of stain or wrinkle- holy and without faults."

(Ephesians 5:25-27 GOD'S WORD)

Fathers, do not exasperate your children; instead, bring them up in the training and instruction of the Lord." Ephesians 6:4.

"For I have chosen him, so that he will direct his children and his household after him to keep the way of the LORD by doing what is right and just, so that the LORD will bring about for Abraham what he has promised him." (Genesis 18:19 NIV)

Another kind of roles assigned to the husband is the spiritual roles of a Priest, a Pastor, a Prophets and a Teacher. Every role that the husband is assigned is also assigned to the wife as his helper. For instance when the husband is wearing his priestly hat as the priest of the family, his wife is the assistance priest.

The Role of the Wife

Whatever role the husband plays, the wife is also expected to play as his assistance. The only difference is that her role is guided by her position as a helper. This is helpful for the smooth operation of the family. A Chinese proverb says that "you can't have two tigers on the same mountain." A ship with two captains is likely to drown. That is why the scripture says;

"22Wives, submit to your own husbands, as to the Lord. 23For the husband is head of the wife, as also Christ is head of the church; and He is the Savior of the body. 24Therefore, just as the church is subject to Christ, so let the wives be to their own husbands in everything." Ephesians 5:22-24.

The 7 Steps to A Successful Marriage

A Wife's primary role is to respect and reverence her husband's leadership. If a wife chooses not to play this role the marriage suffers and may be unable to fulfill its purpose. "Unto the woman he said, I will greatly multiply your sorrow and your conception; in sorrow you shall bring forth children; and your desire shall be to your husband, and he shall rule over you." (Genesis 3:16 KJV)

A Wife's secondary rule is to help her husband pursue their destiny and build their family. "And the LORD God said, "It is not good that the man should be alone; I will make him a helper suitable for him" (Genesis 2:18)

The word helper means the following acronym:

- **H**old her husband daily and keep him stable and focused on the task at hand,
- **E**ncourage him and be his loudest cheerleader especially when he is down or second-guessing himself.
- **L**abor with him in the pursuit of the destiny of the couple
- **P**ray with him and pray for him to succeed in his endeavor.
- **E**mbrace him when the going gets tough and he feels dejected or discouraged.
- **R**escue him when he wanders away from the program or gets himself in trouble.

Every wife opens the door of favor for her husband. This is a spiritual law that does not depend on the wife. "He who finds a wife finds a good thing and obtains favor from the Lord" Proverbs 18:22

The 7 Steps to A Successful Marriage

Please understand that God has given each spouse the grace to fulfill his or her purpose in the marriage. You and your spouse may be former schoolmates, you may be the same age, and you may be more qualified than he is but you are not the husband. Remember that a house divided against it cannot stand. This is a spiritual law that applies to the kingdom of the devil and the kingdom of God. Successful Couples relish their roles in the marriage and play it with zeal.

The 7 Steps to A Successful Marriage

The 7 Steps to A Successful Marriage

Chapter 5
Follow The Process Of Marriage

Ask yourself "What System do I want in My Home?"

...And they shall become one flesh. Gen 2:24.

The fifth step to your Successful Marriage is to follow the process of marriage as set by the Maker of marriage. Folks the word of God is simple and His principles are easy to apply. Jesus Christ said "seek first the kingdom of God, and His righteousness and all these things will be added to you." (Matthew 6:33) The destination of every covenant marriage is oneness between the husband and the wife, but the process is to that oneness is to seek first the Kingdom of God and the rest will be added to us.

I came across Portia Nelson's poem "There is a hole in my Sidewalk" a few years ago. I may have read that poem a zillion times since then and I may still read those five chapters a zillion more times. I am always amazed at how it can simplify our seemingly complicated problems of marriage. I discovered that the problems in marriage follow the same

The 7 Steps to A Successful Marriage

pattern. Each marriage may be unique but the patterns repeat themselves.

The poem goes like this:

There's A Hole In My Sidewalk – by Portia Nelson

Chapter One

> I walk down the street.
> There is a deep hole in the sidewalk.
> I fall in.
> I am lost… I am helpless.
> It isn't my fault.
> It takes forever to find a way out.

Chapter Two

> I walk down the same street.
> There is a deep hole in the sidewalk.
> I pretend I don't see it.
> I fall in again.
> I can't believe I am in the same place.
> But it isn't my fault.
> It still takes a long time to get out.

Chapter Three

> I walk down the same street.
> There is a deep hole in the sidewalk.
> I see it is there.
> I still fall in… it's a habit.
> My eyes are open.
> I know where I am.
> It is my fault… I get out immediately.

Chapter Four

The 7 Steps to A Successful Marriage

I walk down the same street.

There is a deep hole in the sidewalk.

I walk around it.

Chapter Five

I walk down another street.

Although Portia Nelson was talking about her struggles with alcoholic addiction it does resonate with the struggles we face in our marriages. First we feel helpless, then we blame others including our spouse, and then we pretend the problems are not there until they take a deeper grip in our life. Finally our eyes open and some of us find a solution while others are overtaken by the problem. We can avoid the holes in the sidewalks of our marriage if we follow the pathway laid down by the Maker of marriage.

Your marriage has a method to its madness that works for the institution. As in the process of building this is where the depth of your foundation matters. The process of marriage is where you dig deeper; reinforcing the foundation you dug at the beginning of the marriage. Every choice you made before now factors into the process of marriage.

A few years ago, a young lady called me for advice on what to do with her marriage. She met this young man who was living far away from her country and after 2 days of dating the young man proposed and she accepted. Things had to move fast because the young had only three weeks to stay in the country. He must go back to the foreign Country to resume his lucrative job as an engineer with an oil and gas Company. The young man left two weeks later and visited the country twice-in three years for 30 days. She was lucky to get pregnant in those two visits and now have two children. 2 months ago she joined her husband in the foreign country only to find out that the man is a monster. He is selfish and uncaring, immature to the point of running everything he did by his mother and that drove the young lady nuts. She was not allowed to go out on her own or make any phone calls. The last straw that broke the camel's back was that the man who had been verbally abusive finally took it to the next level by hitting her in front of the children. The young lady moved out of the house into a women shelter.

Now she wants advice on what to do. Talk about not laying any foundation at all for her marriage! I asked her why she married this man that she hardly knew that fast? She told me that she thought she was making the right choice. The man was good looking, had a very lucrative job and lived in a foreign country that she has been dreaming of visiting. How do you repair this cracked foundation or this building without foundation?

The process of marriage is like the construction of a building. Just as you can only build on the foundation that you laid for the building, you can only establish your marriage on the foundation that you laid at the beginning of the marriage. The young lady is in serious trouble.

Communication

The scripture tells us that "He who guards his mouth preserves his life, But he who opens wide his lips shall have destruction" (Proverbs 13:3). This is literarily true of our marriage. Communication is the strongest cord that holds marriages together. The ability to communicate our deepest thoughts and feelings in a manner that is clearly understood and accepted is an invaluable skill that rises to the level of an art and should be coveted by every spouse desiring to build a successful marriage.

Please understand that "Your marriage will rise or fall with your communication skills" -Together forever. God's Master Plan for Marriage by Dr. Vic and May Victor. 2012.

Look at the story of a group of men who set out on a grand project of constructing a tower high enough to reach Heaven. Their motive was to make a name for themselves and to prevent their members from dispersing around the earth contrary to God's instruction. At first they made tremendous progress and were on the verge of succeeding with the goal until the Lord came down and confused their language. When they could not communicate with each other, they abandoned the project and scattered all over the world

Notice that at first the men were unstoppable in the pursuit of their project. See what God said about them, "Indeed the people are one and they all have one language, and this is what they begin to do; now nothing that they propose to do will be withheld from them" (Genesis 11:6).

The men succeeded in the project because they could communicate with each and communication made it possible for them to become a team and work in unity. Communication helped them in two particular ways:

1. Unity of Language: Language skills gave them the ability to maintain the unity of purpose. Can you imagine the brick layer asking for brick and getting water, or the foreman calling for a lunch break as the workers continue to work

2. Unity of Purpose: The men had the same goal of making a name for themselves and staying together.

The 7 Steps to A Successful Marriage

When a husband and wife consummate their marriage they seal their marriage covenant with blood and become one. That oneness is irrevocable since no power or process can reverse a covenant that is sealed with blood. Although this oneness is initiated through covenant, it must be maintained through communication and commitment. Note this, the most delicate soft target in your marriage is your marital language and that is why it is a battleground.

Notice what God said about people who have one language and one speech "Nothing which they purpose to do will be impossible". Can you imagine God saying this about you and your spouse if only you can speak the same language with your spouse? The power of speaking the same language is so potent that God could only intervene by confusing the language of the men. Every problem in any marriage is a problem of communication. Communication occurs when there is a meeting of the mind between two or more persons. Two cannot work together except they agree!

The same situation is true of several marriages. At the beginning of each relationship the couples communicate more and enjoy the relationship better. Effective communication helps newly married couples to pursue their projects more efficiently. The project of engagement, wedding, honeymoon and settling down are carried out with ease because of the oneness between the parties.

Unfortunately the languages change soon after and confusion set in. No wonder the unions begin to disintegrate just like the men building the tower of Babel did. One statistics shows that couples communicate with each other for an average of 4-5 hours a day during the period of courtship and dating, but only five minutes after marriage. One woman told me recently that the only communication she had with her husband for the whole day was "I need the blanket".

Here are a few things to note about communication in marriage.

- Words, no matter how many of it we say or how loud we say it means nothing unless it communicates something. (Vain repetition & Noise)
- Just because you are talking does not mean you are communicating.
- Words are 7% of what we are saying; Tone is 38%; Body Language 53%.
- Effective communication allows you to pursue projects and defend the union.

Your ability to communicate with your spouse is a spiritual weapon that works both for you and against you. Every divorce and separation starts from the husband and wife being confused in their speech or lack of speech. First they start disagreeing, and then they start arguing because they do not agree. After that phase they start fighting because they do not understand one another; finally one person moves out because he/she can't bear it. If they retrace their steps they may be able to point out where it all began; the misunderstandings, the disagreements, the arguments and the fights. God uses the power of communication to create things but the devil uses the same power to destroy things.

Intimacy

The Word says that the two shall become one flesh. After you have developed an effective communication skill, the next thing in the process of marriage is to use that communication skill to communicate and understand your spouse. The language skills we acquired will help us to communicate our deepest feelings and exchange information for building that successful marriage. God may have made you for each other but you have to understand each other before you can succeed. It is not enough that you are meant for each other, you have to understand where you complement each other. Your spouse is supposed to compliment you in the areas of your life that you need help and that makes for one formidable team.

The process of oneness is a journey of discovery that starts from courtship and spans through the lifetime of the marriage. I have always known my wife to be an organizer and one who gets things done but I have never appreciated that gift in her as much as I should until during the course of writing this book. It took her only minutes to find out some information that I have searched for countless hours.

The second phase in the process of marriage is to become intimate. The more intimate you are with your spouse the easier it is to survive and even thrive in the world. Intimacy is a deeper level of communication that is exclusive to the couple. An intimate relationship is an interpersonal relationship that involves four areas:

1. **Physical or Emotional Intimacy** is the level of intimacy where the couple understands each other's feelings. Your spouse does not need to say a word before you understand how he/she is feeling. This is an important process in building a successful marriage because what we say is only 7% of what we are saying.

2. **Spiritual Intimacy** is also a higher level of communication and understanding on spiritual matters. One way to notice spiritual intimacy is your communication with God on matters concerning the

marriage and the household. This happens to my wife and I, but the one that happened last year, 2011, is still fresh in my mind. We had decided to leave our local church where we had worship for over 10 years. That decision was made while we were abroad on a missionary outreach. When we came back from that trip, we were set to leave but agreed to continue worshipping in the Church until we found another church. During the first Church service that we attended after returning from the trip, the Lord told me among other things that we should stay in the Church. I was not sure how to tell my wife because all along I was the one pushing for us to leave the church. When we got home that afternoon I finally gathered enough courage to tell her. She looked at me and said, The Lord told me the same thing while we were in the Church. Needless to say, subsequent events confirmed that God wanted us to stay in the Church. Husband and wife are the pastors and co pastors of the church in their house. They must develop the right spiritual chemistry to minister to their household.

3. Social Intimacy is enjoying each other's company. As we saw earlier on one of the purposes of marriage is companionship. If you hate to be around each other or can't get along, it is a sign that you are not building a successful marriage. Most successful couples would rather be with each other fighting than, have fun with anybody else.

4. Intellectual Intimacy is the level of intimacy where you respect each other's intellect whether you appreciate it or not. I am a Phlegmatic-melancholy by character trait but my wife is sanguine-choleric and that is very evident in the way we think. I think outside the box but my wife sees things the way they are. That process of thinking fascinated me at the beginning of our relationship but that quickly became a nightmare after we got married. This continued until we learned to respect each other's intellect. I may not understand it but I sure do respect it now. It's a level of intimacy that allows us to discuss issues and arrive at a solution or conclusion and at the same time building synergy.

While most of us focus on the physical intimacy, I believe that the spiritual intimacy is the glue that holds the other three intimacies together; it is the foundation that makes the union stable and the painting that makes the marriage beautiful. Praying and studying the bible together helps to build the deepest of intimacy.

A man "Leaves his father and mother, cleaves to his wife before they can become one flesh" Sleeping together does not mean you are intimate but it is certainly part of it. Living in the same house does not mean you are intimate with each other but that's part of it too. The longer you know each other the more intimate you are in socialization, sentiments, Spiritual things, and intellect. Presence and focus creates intimacy. Whatever we focus our attention on grows.

Successful marriages are between friends who are willing to continue investing in the friendship. Couples need to get to that point where they can't find comfort with any other person than their spouse. We encourage singles to cultivate friendship before marriage and maintain it through marriage. If you are not friends with your spouse, become one. One of the questions we get all the time in seminars is "How do I become friends with my husband or wife if he/she is not friendly toward me? Our answer is always, make yourself friendly, make time for him/her and be nice to him/her. It works magic because nobody hates receiving kindness.

When a husband and wife are intimate in all four areas, the result is magical. That's when you call your spouse on the phone and he/she says, "I just picked up the phone to call you", or I was just thinking about you. Some call it telepathy but the real thing is that the soul is becoming one. When a team has good understanding we call it chemistry.

Money

The next step in the process of building a successful marriage is to develop and master a common perspective to money. Money is not bad for marriage on its own but how we see money creates conflicts. Money is so important in life and in marriage that it is mentioned 284 times in the bible. Money accounts for over 40% of all the divorces in the US (90% of fights and arguments in marriages). Money can make or break any marriage. Here are a few things the bible tells us about money and how to deal with money.

- A feast is made for laughter, and wine makes life merry, but money is the answer for everything. (Eccl. 10:19)
- Money has been offered to buy the power of God. (Acts 8:18)
- Money has been used to deceive and distract many from pursuing their purpose. "Certainly, the love of money is the root of all kinds of evil. Some people who have set their hearts on getting rich have wandered away from the Christian faith and have caused themselves a lot of grief. (Timothy 6:10 GOD'S WORD)

The 7 Steps to A Successful Marriage

Some of the areas of conflict with money are:

1. Loving money
2. Making money
3. Saving money.
4. Spending money
5. Allocating where to spend money

Money is a tool for building the family. The couple that succeeds in having the same view of money will succeed in all they do.

Renewal and Refreshment

The final phase in the process of building a Successful Marriage is to renew and refresh periodically. Successful Couples understand the importance of the union as a team so they are constantly building up the team and focusing/refocusing on themselves and their purpose. Here are some facts about our marriage.

- We spend 12 years in High School, 4 years in College in other to get a job that we will work for 1/3 of our life. (Most people work for 20-30 life on their job) But we spend only three weeks of premarital counseling for a marriage that we intend to last for a 2/3 of our life.
- The irony of life is that those couples who are doing well in their marriage keep renewing and rejuvenating their marriage while those who really need to relearn certain things never attend seminars, conferences, or even read any book on marriage.

There are five ways we build our marriage

The 7 Steps to A Successful Marriage

1. **University of Mom and Dad.** This is the primary education for marriage that we attend long before we think of marriage. The things we learn here form our beliefs in marriage. Those spouses from parents whose marriage were successful have the tendency to want to prefer the same prototype for their family.

2. **Pre-Marital Counseling.** This a crash course of about 3-6 weeks depending on which church you is involved with. You learn a lot here but not enough to keep your marriage.

3. **Books, tapes, Seminars and Conferences.** This is the most effective ongoing avenue for getting information about marriage. The challenge is to find the right one. Recently my wife and I attended two marriage seminars in one weekend. Dr. Gary Chapman hosted one of them and The Redeemed Christian Church of God hosted the other. At the Garry Chapman conference we relearned the five-love language. a. Words of affirmation, b. Acts of service, c. Gift, d. Quality time and Physical touch. It was refreshing and informative.

4. **Mentors/Mentees and Peers.** Mentors are valuable source of information and support for marriages. Most successful couples have both formal and informal mentors, you should have one too. Couples who have mentors that they model their relationship after are successful.

5. **Renewals and vacations.** This is the most important way to build the union. Setting aside "US" time is very important. In my house we do it both spontaneously and scheduled. The key is to make time.

The 7 Steps to A Successful Marriage

The 7 Steps to A Successful Marriage

Chapter 6
Set Boundaries For Your Marriage And Defend It

Ask yourself, "Who are the members of my family?"

Jesus Christ taught the principle of focus and the dilemma of an unfocused life. He said "No one can serve two masters; for either he will hate the one and love the other, or else he will be loyal to the one and despise the other. You cannot serve God and mammon." (Matthew 6:24) We can extrapolate from this statement that you cannot serve your destiny and the destinies of your friends and families at the same time. Any attempt to do so will pitch you in between the two interests. The wise thing is to follow your destiny because it is by serving your destiny that the destinies of your friends, your families and foes are served. Your destiny is the same as your path in the kingdom of God.

The 7 Steps to A Successful Marriage

The sixth step to a successful marriage is to set boundaries around your marriage and protect it 24/7. Don't assume that all your friends, your family members and your foes including all those who attended your wedding wish your marriage success. Those people who made that assumption live to regret it. This is very important for your bonding as husband and wife and in maintaining the culture, sanctity and routine of the new family. Never assume that everyone related to you by blood or friendship is necessarily related to you by destiny and purpose. If it were so the Lord would not have asked you to leave them behind.

"Therefore a man shall leave his father and mother and be joined to his wife and they shall be one." (Genesis 2:24)

Please understand that in relation to building boundaries for your marriage:

- The members of your household are your wife, children and you. Every other person is a stranger.
- When God wants to elevate a man he separates him from his people and place.
- Separate your destiny partners from your destiny helpers. Destiny helpers are outside your ring of destiny of God.
- There are only enough provisions for your partners and none for your helpers.
- The LORD had said to Abram, Leave your country, your people and your father's household and go to the land I will show you. Genesis 12:1-4, Genesis 13:7-8, 10, Genesis 19:36-37. Micah 7:5-6.
- People come into your house with their bodies, souls and spirits. Beware whom you open your doors for.

- Leave them alone. God has a reason for commanding us to leave our father and mother. If He says leave your father and mother, He implied your friends too. You have enough baggage where you are going to add more to yourself.
- Everything you do has to be for the best interest of the union.

In Genesis 12:1, Abraham was given a clear instruction to

"Go from your country and your kindred and your father's house to the land that I will show you. And I will make of you a great nation, and I will bless you and make your name great, so that you will be a blessing. I will bless those who bless you, and him who dishonors you I will curse, and in you all the families of the earth shall be blessed."

Notice that Abraham was instructed to take only what belonged to him for this journey and to leave behind everything that is jointly owned or shared with his countrymen, kindred and brethren. Throughout the bible we see that whenever God wanted to elevate or advance a man He separates him from his past, his people and his present because separation leads to isolation; isolation leads to revelation and revelation leads to elevation. Separation is therefore the prerequisite for elevation from a foot soldier to a general in the kingdom of God. God separates us when he wants to assign us to a specific job but we must separate ourselves when we desire to be a general in His army.

Now let's see how much of God's instruction that Abraham obeyed. Keep in mind that partial obedience is total disobedience.

"So Abram went, as the LORD had told him, and Lot went with him. Abram was seventy-five years old when he departed from Haran. And Abram took Sarai his wife, and Lot his brother's son, and all their possessions that they had gathered, and the people that they had acquired in Haran, and they set out to go to the land of Canaan." (Genesis 12:4)

Notice again that Abraham departed as he was instructed but Lot 'imposed' himself on Abraham and the vision. ...And Lot went with him" means that Lot volunteered himself to go with Abraham. From the moment that Lot came into the picture, the adjective changed from "He and his" to "they and their". Abraham had to take Lot's belongings, burdens and baggage.

Nothing changes the landscape of a man's destiny faster than comingling of Spirits, souls and bodies that have no business being together. It is said that opposites attract in life, but in the Spirit realm, opposites repel. Now let's look at some of the consequences of that costly gaffe by Abraham:

- Provision in the land was not enough for both Abraham and Lot. Abraham gave out the choice area of the land to Lot for the sake of peace. Lot was moving around with Abram. Lot also had flocks and herds and tents. But the land didn't have enough food for both of them. They had large herds and many servants. So they weren't able to stay together. The people who took care of Abraham's herds and those who took care of Lot's

herds began to argue. Genesis 13:5-7 - In other to resolve this conflict between his people and Lot's people Abraham chose peace over conflict.
- Lot's herdsmen quarreled with Abraham's herdsmen over the scarce provision and that conflict almost involved Abraham and Lot.
- Lot chose the best place in the Land and Abraham was left with the less fertile land.

Lot looked up. He saw that the whole Jordan River valley had plenty of water. It was like the garden of the Lord. It was like the land of Egypt near Zoar. That was before the Lord destroyed Sodom and Gomorrah.

So Lot chose the whole Jordan River valley for himself. Then he started out toward the east". (Gen. 13:9-11)

- Abraham fought a war to free Lot from King Chedorlaomer who took Lot and his household captive. This was the only war that Abraham fought. 14Now when Abram heard that his brother was taken captive, he armed his three hundred and eighteen trained servants who were born in his own house, and went in pursuit as far as Dan. 15He divided his forces against them by night, and he and his servants attacked them and pursued them as far as Hobah, which is north of Damascus. 16So he brought back all the goods, and also brought back his brother Lot and his goods, as well as the women and the people. Genesis 14:14-16
- Abraham had to intervene to save Lot from the Angels of God during the destruction of Sodom and Gomorrah. 23 And Abraham came near and said, "Would You also

destroy the righteous with the wicked? 24Suppose there were fifty righteous within the city; would You also destroy the place and not spare it for the fifty righteous that were in it? 25Far be it from You to do such a thing as this, to slay the righteous with the wicked, so that the righteous should be as the wicked; far be it from You! Shall not the Judge of all the earth do right?"26So the Lord said, "If I find in Sodom fifty righteous within the city, then I will spare all the place for their sakes." (Gen 18:23-26) His negotiation skills and grace was stretched to the max to save Lot and his household.

- Lot was the father of the Moabites and the Ammonites who became Israel's archenemies till today and lured the Israelite into worshipping idols. 36Thus both the daughters of Lot were with child by their father. 37The firstborn bore a son and called his name Moab; he is the father of the Moabites to this day. 38And the younger, she also bore a son and called his name Ben-Ammi; he is the father of the people of Ammon to this day. (Genesis 19:36-38.)

We often commingle our destiny with the destinies of other people especially the members of our extended family and our close friends without knowing the Spirits that control those people. One classic example is in marriage. When a women gets married in Africa they are expected to take a younger sibling along to the husband's house primarily as a way of helping the family. Understand that your younger sibling is not necessarily going where you are going. She may be blood but she may not share the blood of Jesus Christ. She may even share the blood of Jesus Christ but may not share your assignment.

The 7 Steps to A Successful Marriage

Every newlywed in Israel is allowed to take one-year honeymoon, leave and vacation. During this time the couple is exempt from draft into the army and from going to war if he was already a soldier. The idea is for the husband and wife to bond together and forge their own future/determine their destiny. This is a custom that has been there from the beginning and approved by the scriptures. (Deuteronomy 24:5)

These days, you are lucky if you have three days honey moon. One couple told me that her husband took her to his sister's house in New Jersey for their honey moon and while there she was expected to do chores and run errands in the house. Honeymoon is a time for just the husband and the wife to focus on each other alone.

Although Abraham made the mistake of his life and suffered the consequences, he learned his lessons from then onward. When the Lord gave him another opportunity he made sure that his obedience was complete. The bible says that the Lord tested Abraham again by asking him to sacrifice his only son. Abraham took his son Isaac, two of his servants on his way to the place that the Lord had revealed to him for the sacrifice but not all the way.

"Then on the third day, Abraham lifted up his eyes and saw the place afar off. And Abraham said to the young men, Stay here with the donkey; I and the lad will go yonder and worship, and we will come back to you" It sounds like Abraham was saying, "this is for family only and you are not family". (Genesis 22:5-6)

We often underestimate the power of our friends to distract us and overestimate the ability of our enemies to deter us. The truth is that our enemies spur us on while our friends distract us. Distracters get all the credit and none of the blames.

The 7 Steps to A Successful Marriage

Have you ever heard anybody blaming his mother or father or friends for not becoming important in life, or for not getting that promotion or getting that grade. We just don't look that close to home but the advice of a mother and the influence of a friend are more impactful than the arrow of an enemy. Distracters do more to stifle our dreams than any other person.

No wonder the prophet Micah said that "a man's enemies are members of his household." (Micah 7:6). Jesus Christ was quick to distance himself from the notion that his mother and blood brothers share his destiny and vision. He took that opportunity to teach his disciples that a visionary's families are those who share his vision. History has shown that your blood brothers are the least excited about your vision and progress. The brothers of Joseph mocked him and derided his dream of being great. The sons of Jesse wondered why David came to the war front at all. Jesus was ineffective in his birthplace.

Beloved, understand that there are three kinds of people in our destiny team. The moment we recognize this is the moment our destiny takes a life of its own. Identifying each person in your team makes for a coercive team; and that ultimately will help you reach your kingdom. Each of the people is identified by the roles they play in the team and not necessarily by their names or consanguinity.

Note that the roles of the team members change from time to time and from project to project. A destiny partner in one vision may become a destiny helper in another project and a destiny killer in another instance depending on their personal interest and understanding. Mariam was a lifesaver for Moses, a partner for his vision but later became a destiny hater. She even questioned Moses calling and authority. Job's wife was a destiny helper by marriage but became a destiny hater when she advised Job to "curse God and die".

The three members of your destiny team are:

Destiny Partners

These are the people you share your destiny and destination with. You may not have the same origin or share the same biological bloodline but you share the same destination and the same spiritual bloodline. Your wife is your destiny partner and destiny helper. Your children are not necessarily your destiny partners. Isaac had two children but only Jacob was part of his destiny and dynasty. God had a different plan for Esau and he became a nation in his own right. Jacob had twelve sons but only Judah was part of the plan of God for Abraham's dynasty. The rest of the children had a different destiny.

Ishmael's birth was neither an unplanned birth nor was he an illegitimate child; but he was not in the plan of God for Abraham. Ishmael was a casualty of Sarah's mistrust and impatience. She wanted it faster than God planned it so God granted her wishes. Ishmael and Hagar were not sent away because Hagar was a slave woman and Ishmael was the son of a bondwoman, they were sent away because they were not part of the original plan. Destiny is the divine plan of God for every man.

Again in the story of Judah we see the near destruction of his destiny. "Judah went away from his brothers and visited a friend of his, a certain Adullamite whose name was Hirah. While there Judah saw a woman from the city whose name was Shua. He married her as his wife and lived with her" Genesis 38:1-2. Note the phrase "a certain" indicates that the two persons mentioned there, Hirah and Shua were nobodies as far the plan of God was concerned until now.

Judah did the same thing that Esau the son of Isaac did; they both went outside the bloodline in disobedience to the plan of God. Judah was later restored into the plan of God but Esau who was never in line to inherit the promise made to Abraham was never recovered. Why you may ask? The answer is Destiny and destiny partners. Esau was destined to be less than Jacob no matter how much he tried. Judah was destined to be the destiny carrier, the promise keeper of the Abrahamic covenant and the most enduring tribe of Judah no matter how much he messed up.

Destiny Helpers

Your destiny helpers are people placed in your life to help you with your destiny. Their role in your life is to provide whatever you are lacking and to lift you up whenever you need help. They do their job willingly and perfectly. They are not your armor bearers as some say; they are part of your arsenals for overcoming your challenges. They understand the vision even before the vision is clear to the you, the visioner. Note how the bible described Jonathan, David's destiny Helper. "And it came to pass, when he had finished speaking unto Saul that the soul of Jonathan was knit with the soul of David, and Jonathan loved him as his own soul". (1 Samuel 18:1)

They usually show up like saviors, work for you like faithful servants and exit the scene like angels. Their life revolves around the vision as if the vision is theirs. The duration of their job is short and definite. Every destiny carrier has a destiny helper. They are not always your friends but they are the provision for your vision. In the case of your marriage it could be the friend or the person that helped you met your spouse. It could be the man or woman who took over your weeding expense or arrangement or the pastor or mentor that helped you through a rough time in your marriage. It is important to note that a destiny partner may become a destiny helper and a destiny helper may become a destiny hater. Destiny helpers are notorious for over staying their welcome, overstepping their boundaries and demanding for a pound of flesh. Appreciate them and what they are doing or have done for you but understand their role. In the end, give God thanks for their presence in your life. Remember they are helpers and not partners.

Destiny Haters

A destiny hater is one who delays, detours, distracts or destroys your destiny. They are usually easy to spot because of their loud mouth and mean acts toward your marriage, your choice of spouse, the place where your spouse is from, your spouse family, profession, the timing of your marriage or simple hatred and discouragement for anything concerning marriage. They do not keep their feelings to themselves. Sometime they are subtle, pretending to be helpful but ceasing every opportunity you offer them to discourage you from the marriage. They are at work, your unmarried friends, siblings, parents and strangers. Please understand that they have an agenda and that is to delay, detour, distract and destroy your marriage. Anybody or anything that is tearing you apart from your spouse or your marriage is not a friend of your marriage. Beware of destiny helpers that turn into destiny haters. Those are the most dangerous because they know you better than you know yourself. These are the best friend that you think are helping you resolve the issues in your marriage but turn out to have their own agenda.

When you identify these kinds of people around you, it is easier to set boundaries and protect the palace 24/7.

Chapter 7

Hunker Down For The Long Journey

The number "7" is the symbol of completion and fullness. The seventh step to a successful marriage is to hunker down for the life long journey. Marriage is a marathon and not a sprint. Like every marathon its success is not measured by where you are in the race or how fast you are running at the moment but marriage is measured by the race you are running. Are you running your race or are the other couples forcing you to run their race?

Avoid Distractions

More often than not we start well in marriage, on a solid foundation, with the right purpose in our heart but other couples distract us. I heard the story of a married woman who met a young man on the Facebook. Subsequently she travelled overseas to meet this young man and stayed with him for weeks. When she eventually came back from the trip she filed for divorce and served her husband with the papers. At the moment the story is still unfolding but there you see a classic case of distractions from the devil. You don't need to be a rocket scientist to predict that the boy will use this woman and dump her as soon as she helps him come to America. This story underscores how we can be distracted from pursuing our destiny, deceived from focusing on our purpose and convinced to abandon our covenant relationship.

It is not unusual to hear people talk about their marital woes and marital bliss to people they hardly know. Time and time again people who have gone through divorce or separation advise younger men and women going through challenges in their marriage to get out of it. They paint a picture of a rosy and easier life as a single person or as a single parent. They talk about the independence they are supposedly enjoying. My heart bleeds each time I hear these false testimonials because you can spot the lies from a distance. The life they are portraying is far from the life they are living. Please understand that most single parents are having a tough time raising their children by themselves and living their lives alone. If it was easy being single God would not have said that it is not good for Adam to be alone. You know the statics for divorce is very high but the statistics for those desiring to get married is higher. That tells me that more people want to get married than those desiring to get out of marriage.

Success in marriage comes from running your own race, maintaining your own pace and keeping your eyes on the price and the principle. It is your destiny, your purpose and your covenant, do not compromise it by listening to those who have already messed up their own marriage or those whose marriage is doing good under a different destiny

The 7 Steps to A Successful Marriage

There is no doubt that marriage is a lifetime hard work. Marriage is not based on the principle of fairness. It demands 100% from you and 100% from your spouse. You cannot excuse yourself from not doing your part on the ground that your spouse is not doing his/her part. That may be acceptable in contract, but marriage is not a contract. Marriage is an irrevocable covenant.

What else could be harder than making a lifetime commitment to stay with the same person every day for the rest of your life? We often forget that marriage is 24/7, 365 days, no vacation, no timeout and no leave of absence. Even when you are sleeping you are still married and doing marriage.

See you and your spouse in 20 years from now, 25 years from now and even 50 years from now, enjoying your retirement with your grandchildren and your children in the mist. Never see yourself as a separate entity or alone in your future plan. My wife and I have made the decision that the "D" word does not exist in our household.

The 7 Steps to A Successful Marriage

Chapter 8

The 5 Steps To Remaking A Messed-Up Marriage

A young woman called us for advice after one of our television broadcasts. She came to the United States under the visa lottery program of the State Department. That program allows a certain number of immigrants to live in the United States every year. Each country has a certain number of visas allocated to them. That number of visa is distributed to the citizens of the country who qualify through a lottery system. When this young woman came she knew only one friend in the Unites States and it was her first time of coming to the United States. Her friend offered her accommodation and feeding but rarely had time to take her around and teach her the ropes.

After sitting at home for two months she got a job and through the job she met another immigrant who agreed to give her a ride to work and back from work. A few weeks after meeting the guy she agreed to date him after many days of constant pressure. Although she did not particularly have any feeling for the guy, she felt like that's her only way of appreciating him for all the things he was doing for her. Besides she felt sorry for the guy.

Then the guy suggested she move into one of the bedrooms in his apartment to make it easier for them to ride together to work and she accepted. It seemed like a good idea since she was spending most night in the apartment already. He promised her that he will marry her in a year when he is done with school.

At first everything was going well and they even started trying to have a baby together. Then one day he went out and came back to the apartment with another woman. When she complained to him he simply told her to remember that they were not yet married adding that the way things were he doubts if the marriage will work out between them. The young lady was devastated. She felt violated, used and now abused to say the least but she stayed because she had nowhere else to go but her heart was broken. At this time she had grown to love him and had conditioned her mind to marry him. To make matters worse the guy advised her to make plans to move out before his wife joins him from his country of origin. Now this young lady wants to know what she should do with her life.

The principles of building or rebuilding are the same except that when you are rebuilding there are additional preparation to be done. Whether you started your marriage on the wrong foundation or you started on the right foundation but continued with the wrong materials the process of rebuilding is the same.

It starts from the mindset of the person and proceeds to the actual building. The state of the heart of a person is very important because like every construction, you have to remove the dirt and the debris of the previous foundation before replacing it with a new foundation. Most battles for rebuilding a foundation are lost at this fragile state when the person is fighting to reject the old lifestyle and replace it with a new lifestyle. If you win the battle here, you are more likely to win the war. If you follow the steps laid out here you increase your chances of winning the battle.

Stephen R. Covey once wrote that, "Correct principles are like compasses: they are always pointing the way. And if we know how to read them, we won't get lost, confused or fooled by <u>conflicting voices and values</u>. Principles are self-evident, self-validating natural laws. They don't change or shift. They provide the true "north direction" to our lives when navigating the streams of our environment. Principles apply at all times and in all places. They surface in form of <u>value</u>, <u>ideas</u>, <u>norm</u> and teaching that <u>uplift</u>, <u>ennoble</u>, <u>fulfill</u>, <u>empower</u> and <u>inspire</u> people". Principle Centered Leadership Page 19.

Nehemiah, one of the maverick rebuilders of his time offers us five great principles for building and rebuilding anything including marriages.

1. Conviction or Concern

Every building starts with a decision just as every rebuilding starts with a conviction or concern. There is no repentance without realization and no enlightenment without light. It is the entrance of His word that gives light. The bible says that the prodigal son "came to himself" or "came to his senses" and started some self-talk. Luke 15:17. The phrase "came to him," suggests that prior to that time the prodigal son was not himself. He was not himself when he thought about asking his father for a share of his wealth. He was not himself when he packed his belonging and left his father's house for another country. He was not himself when he squandered his inheritance. If he was not himself it means that he was living a lie as they say in the local parlance here in Texas. If he could live all that lie and for that long and still be forgiven, it means there is hope for all of us. I love what Job said about conviction and rebuilding.

> Submit to God and be at peace with him;
> In this way prosperity will come to you.
> Accept instruction from his mouth
> And lay up his words in your heart.
>
> If you return to the Almighty, you will be restored:
> If you remove wickedness far from your tent
> And assign your nuggets to the dust,
> Your gold of Ophir to the rocks in the ravines,
> Then the Almighty will be your gold,
> The choicest silver for you.
>
> Surely then you will find delight in the Almighty
> And will lift up your face to God.
> You will pray to him, and he will hear you,
> And you will fulfill your vows.
> What you decide on will be done,
> And light will shine on your ways.
> When men are brought low and you say, 'Lift them up!'
> Then he will save the downcast.
> He will deliver even one who is not innocent,
> Who will be delivered through the cleanness of your hands.
>
> (Job 22:21-30 NIV)

Notice that it said "You will pray to him and he will hear you and you will fulfill your vows" What a profound assurance that by returning or turning from our status quo we are guaranteed of the Lord's attention.

Likewise having a conviction that the foundation of your marriage is faulty; that the process of your marriage is wrong; or that you are not playing your God given role in your marriage; or that you have not built enough protective boundaries for your marriage is the beginning of rebuilding your marriage. Being concerned about the way your covenant marriage is going is the first step to doing it right. Is. 6:5-8, Nehemiah 1:3-4.

Understanding is a critical step to making it right. For instance accepting your role in the marriage is a prerequisite to playing the role. There is nothing the Lord cannot do when we come to him in humility. I have a general advice that I give every "hopeless" case that I have dealt with. Rebuild your relationship with God first and see where He takes you.

2. Confession or Declaration

"For with the heart one believes unto righteousness, and with the mouth confession is made unto salvation." (Romans 10:10). True confessions come from a convicted heart. Genuine confessions are almost and always spontaneous and unashamed. Isaiah 6:5. Again the prodigal son came to himself and said, 'What am I doing here?' Every construction and reconstruction starts with a declaration or confession of intent. The foundation of your marriage was laid with such words as your public vows to be married and your private promises to each other. In the same way the rebuilding process must start with confessions and declaration. When you determine that your marriage is not headed in the right direction or did not start from the right place tell somebody and keep saying it to yourself. The bible says that,

20A man's stomach shall be satisfied from the fruit of his mouth; from the produce of his lips he shall be filled. 21Death and life are in the power of the tongue, and those who love it will eat its fruit. Proverbs 18:20-21

Ideally you want to tell your spouse and bring him/her to see the marriage the way you are seeing it. It does make it easier in the rebuilding process to have both parties on the same page. However it is not the end of the world if he does not see what you are seeing. Continue in the process of remaking your marriage and by the grace of God your good deeds will win him over. Please understand that it is much harder when you are doing the makeover alone.

3. Commitment or Dedication

In the realm of ideas everything depends on enthusiasm… in the real world all rests on perseverance. - Johann Wolfgang von Goethe. Isaiah confessed his shortcomings and immediately committed to being a new prophet with a new message. The prodigal son said "I will arise and go to my father". The commitment phase is where the rubber meets the road. Many builders fail here and many rebuilders abandon the project here. The question is, "How can we go pass this phase of death"? What can we do to avoid stalling? If you have made a commitment to rebuild the wrong or fallen foundations, it is imperative that you stand your ground and build. One way to stay focused on your commitment is to write down all your commitments and broadcast it to as many people as you need to hold you accountable. "Write the vision and make it plain on tablets, that he may run who reads it". Habakkuk 2:2. When visions are written and made plain they take on their own life and speak for themselves. Visions raise up destiny helpers and partners that are independent of you. Make it plain to your family members and friends. Let them know that you are rebuilding the foundation of your marriage, reconstructing the boundaries that you have crossed before, raising the tabernacle of praise and worship in your house, taking on your responsibilities in your family, loving the wife of your youth and submitting to your husband as the scriptures says. This is where you institute a paradigm shift and disassociate with people from the old.

Never do your due diligence before the commitment phase. The school of business teaches you how to count your cost before you commit to a project. The school of the spirit teaches you to commit to your cause before you count your cost. You have to be aware of the project but you can't focus too much on the project. Take it one day at a time. If you fall, get up and continue the process.

4. Caution or Diligence

The lazy man does not roast what he took in hunting, but diligence is man's precious possession. Proverbs 12:26-28.

He who has a slack hand becomes poor, but the hand of the diligent makes rich. Proverbs 10:3-5, Proverbs 12:24.

The hand of the diligent will rule, but the lazy man will be put to forced labor. Proverbs 12:23-25, Proverbs 13:4.

The soul of a lazy man desires, and has nothing. But the soul of the diligent shall be made rich. Proverbs 13:3-5, Proverbs 21:5;

The plans of the diligent lead surely to plenty, but those of everyone who is hasty, surely to poverty. Proverbs 21:5; Proverbs 27:23

Be diligent to know the state of your flocks, and attend to your herds Proverbs 27:22-24.

Evaluate your situation thoroughly before you start rebuilding your marriage and your relationship. Make sure you are in the right frame of mind to start and finish the process.

5. Courage or Boldness

What is Courage? Courage means bravery, boldness, fearlessness, mettle, fortitude, or intrepidity. It is the ability to confront fear, pain, danger, uncertainty, or intimidation- Wikipedia. One the more remarkable examples of courage in the bible was about four young girls who defied the norm and by so doing changed the law and the way business was done in Israel ever. The story is that there was a man in Israel who had four daughters and no son before he died. When the Israelite arrive in the Promised Land and it was time to allocate the land the girls knew that they were about to be homeless since their father had no male child to retain his inheritance. The law in Israel before this story was that women were not entitled to inheritance from their father's estate. Knowing that this law meant that they will be disinherited from their father's estate, these four daughters of Zelophedad approached Moses and demanded that the law be changed to accommodate them. Moses was not inclined to change the law for their sake but the Lord told Moses to change the Law and give them their father's estate. Numbers 27:1-10. This girls changed the cause of history through their courage and boldness.

The 7 Steps to A Successful Marriage

Courage is the strength to stand up when it's easier to fall down and lose hold. It is the conviction to explore new horizons when it's easier to settle for the status quo. I remember Phinehas the son of Eleazar whose bravery and courage pleased the Lord and saved the lives of many Israelites. Numbers 25:4-11. I pray God for the courage to start the rebuilding process today and now. You can do it!

Chapter 9 Epilogue

In 2004, my marriage was in serious trouble. My wife and I were making good money but we were unhappy with each other. Every little thing led to arguments and every argument led to silent treatment that lasted for days, sometimes for weeks. It seemed as if we were competing for who will give the longest silent treatment. It was very obvious to us that our spiritual life was in as much trouble as our personal life but we did not connect the two events. We were so busy with work and our profession that we had no time to pause and fix our leaking roof. I was miserable and my wife was even more miserable because we had created our own world. Every trouble in that world magnified our personal trouble. When that civil war started in our world, we had nobody to run to, and nowhere to go. Who are we going to complain to when everybody around us wished they were us. How do we complain to the pastor when we were marriage ministers and counselors?

Even in that state of unhappiness many still admired us because we still did things together. What people did not know was that the joy of doing things together was not there. We had been together and done thing together for so long that we did not know any other way to go about life. In a way that was a blessing but at that time it was painful to me. One day, I did not want to go home after work, but I did not know where to go. I got into my car and drove around on the freeway for about 45 minutes. At the end I realized that I was heading toward my house without consciously deciding to go home. I was very frustrated. I started wondering and listing what other men did after work? They go to sports bar, they go to their friends, and they go to a restaurant to eat. None those things appealed to me.

People interpret doing things together as closeness, having material wealth as happiness and our past as present. It was the loneliest time of our life. Prior to that time our lives were very triangular from home to work, to church and back home. The problem at home escalated to problems at work. I dreaded going home after work for another bout of arguments. I thought about separation and divorce several times and all the vibes I was getting from my wife was that she did not care one way or the other what happened.

One early morning we argued so much that I started making a mental note of what it will take to get a divorce, the cost and consequences of divorce. We were used to getting up early, sometimes as early as 4 am to talk and pray but by this time even our prayer and bible study time always ended up in arguments. Finally I told my wife to pray by herself and for herself while I did the same. As trained lawyers, we both knew the cost and consequences of divorce and separation, but I was not in the right frame of mind to calculate the spiritual cost. As I thought further into how it will affect our positions in the church and in the society, it downed on me that I had not considered the spiritual implications. Our effort to stop the arguments and recreate the life we had before made it worse. We took out time for short vacations, date nights and even exchanging gifts all to no avail. We were both trying very hard to reclaim our marriage but the more we tried the more we drifted apart.

One morning as I lay awake, thinking and wondering how to deal with the crisis in my marriage, I wondered where God was while this was happening to us and how my divorce will affect my children. I reminisced on how I met wife, the plans we had for our life, our wedding, our friends and what our parents will say. I remember thinking for a minute whether I will ever marry again and who to marry. I remember being overwhelmed by the whole situation. Then thought about how we had drifted away from God and the manual for marriage. Although we were still in the Church but the Church was not really in us.

In fact we were still as active in our church as we both taught bible studies every Sunday morning. We drove the same car to church, sat in the same pew and participated in the church service as usual but we knew we were far from God. To the casual onlooker everything looked perfect. I had a law practice while my wife who is also a lawyer and a registered nurse worked in one of the local hospitals. Our children were doing Ok and we had just moved into the house of our dreams, 4,300 square feet, in a middle class neighborhood with all the trapping of good living but we were unhappy. Then we made the decisions that saved our marriage and invariably our spiritual life. One day we sat down and talked as we had done several times before. There was something different with this talk; we discussed objectively, identified the problems with our marriage and came up with some working solutions as follows:

1. We identified our jobs as the number one culprit after the devil. We both agreed that our marriage was suffering because we were too busy with our jobs. We

figured that it was time to choose between our jobs and our marriage and family. We choose our marriage but it was not easy. Remember we did not trust each other at this time so we had concerns about given up one job and working together.

2. My wife offered to quit her job and join me in the law office. This was the most difficult decision we had ever made to save our marriage. My wife was making a good money and her income was the more stable of the two incomes. The down side of my wife's job was that she worked at night and long hours. On the other hand choosing to keep the Law Office was not easy. Although we made money from the law practice, the overhead of running a law office was a huge discouragement. Besides the income from the law Office was not steady and nothing is guaranteed. In the end we decided to keep the law office.

1. Apart from the disadvantages discussed above we decided that since the priority was to make time for ourselves, the law office gave us the best opportunity to control our destiny and make our schedule. I have always believed that the serpent would not have deceived Eve if Adam was in the house. If we were going to reclaim our lives we had to prioritize our marriage above every other thing.

2. We knew that the process of rebuilding must start with the altar and that we cannot rebuild our marriage without rebuilding the family altar. We knew that every time that something was rebuilt in bible it started with rebuilding the altar. Nehemiah 3:1, 1 Sam 30:1-8. With this in mind we embarked on rebuilding the church in our house. Our family altar had been damaged by months of argument and bickering.

3. We took out time to pray, fast and study the bible. Then we scheduled our Morning Prayer times and started searching the bible for instruction on how to stay married. At the beginning we committed only 30 minutes a day to our devotion time; then we increased it to one hour and thereafter we could not keep count of the time we spent in His presence. We were so excited about what we were discovering in the bible and the new life that we were building that sometimes we woke up at 3am to pray and study the bible.
4. The more we learned the more we applied the word of God to our marriage. We studied the role of marriage in the plan of God, our individual role in the marriage and our commitment to our spouses. As we continued to build up our family altar and fellowship with God, our relationship was healed, our marriage was repaired and our family was stabilized.
5. It was from those early morning hours in the presence of God that our ministry was revealed and restored; our personal life repaired and our marriage healed. We knew we were called into ministry but our commitment to the calling was not what it should be. From the notes we made during those hours we wrote our first book, "Together for Ever, God's Master Plan marriage".

The 7 Steps to A Successful Marriage

The 7 Steps to A Successful Marriage

To order additional copies of

The 7 Steps to A Successful Marriage

Visit the author's website at:

www.twogetherforever.org

Other Books by Authors

Together For Ever,

God's Master Plan For Marriage

To contact the authors:

Email: info@twogether4ever.org

Visit the author's website at:

www.twogether4ever.org

Made in the USA
Columbia, SC
14 September 2024